Becoming

A Person Of Legacy

By: Dr. Delron Shirley

© 2018

Delron Shirley
3210 Cathedral Spires Dr.
Colorado Springs, CO 80904
www.teachallnationsmission.com
teachallnations@msn.com

Table of Contents

Book Cover Photos

Front Cover – My Grandfather and his legacy family

Back Cover – My Grandfather

Preface

This volume is part of a trilogy of short independent works that are intended to stand alone but should also be read as a series since they have a unifying theme. Good People, Bad Things, and Vice Versa deals with the age-old question of why God allows bad things to happen to good people and good things to happen to bad people; the sequel, A New Dawn Rises, deals with the struggles that we go through as Christians, and the concluding volume, Becoming a Person of Legacy, suggests an approach to living a life that makes a lasting mark in history. The consistent thread that is woven throughout the fiber of each book is the biblical principle that a man is what he thinks about in his heart (Proverbs 23:7) and that we have to determine not to be forced into the mold of thinking like everyone else does (Romans 12:2) – hence, the tile: The Non-Conformer's Trilogy.

Introduction

William Carey – after being told to sit down and shut up – eventually won the privilege to stand up before the top leadership of the British churches and convince them that it was the responsibility of European Christians to evangelize the "heathen" of lands they had colonized. A few months later, he was off to India where he would spend the next forty-one years translating the Bible into thirty-four Indian languages; compiling dictionaries of Sanskrit, Marathi, Panjabi, and Telegu; founding the still influential Serampore College; establishing churches and nineteen mission stations; planting more than one hundred rural schools; encouraging the education of girls; starting the Horticultural Society of India; serving as a professor at Fort William College; beginning the weekly publication The Friend of India; printing the first Indian newspaper; introducing the concept of the savings bank to assist poor farmers; and fighting against sati, the burning of widows. As I sat in his chair in Calcutta, the enormity of the legacy of this "Father of Modern Missions" weighed heavily upon me.

I was equally moved by the privilege to stand in the pulpit of Adoniram Judson, the "Father of American Missions" who similarity convinced the churches in America that they had not only the obligation but also the honor of taking the gospel to foreign soil. He set out to India with the support of the American Congregational Churches; however, when his biblical studies convinced him that he should be baptized by immersion, he relinquished that sponsorship and ventured to Burma where – in spite of spending time in prison and the loss of two wives – he was able to translate the Bible into the Burmese language, partially complete a Burmese-English dictionary, establish one hundred churches, and confirm over eight thousand believers.

Of course, the impact of Mark Buntain's legacy was almost overwhelming when I was invited to dine and even spend the night in the apartment of this pioneer Assemblies of God missionary to Calcutta where his thirty-five years of ministry have produced more than eight hundred churches, an entire educational system, several Bible colleges, a hospital, a nurse's training college, and a teacher's college.

When I was first impressed to write about legacy, my mind immediately flashed back to these and other encounters I have been privileged to have with the legacies of men and women who have changed the world. As I began to study the topic, I realized that legacy is not so much about what we do or what we physically leave behind as it is about who we are and what DNA we deposit into the lives of future generations. Without the root of a strong inner personality, we cannot bear the fruit of outward accomplishments and influences. We'll begin our study by looking at the lives of two individuals in ancient Israel who seemed to leave a larger-than-life legacy on the following generations of their nation. In them we will see how the root of their inner personalities determined the fruit of their legacies – one in an incredibly positive way and one in an equally remarkable negative way. David was a godly king who became what we might consider the "gold standard" against which all the succeeding kings were to be measured. On the other end of the spectrum was Jeroboam, who became the villainous role model for the future depravity of his nation. From there, the lessons that I wish to share with you in the next few pages are basically about how to develop our inner man.

David

God asked one requirement of Solomon when He established him on the throne of his father David – that he walk according to the legacy that his father had established. (I Kings 3:14, 9:4, 11:38) However, Solomon failed to do so (I Kings 11:6) and set in motion a pattern that was to differentiate all future generations in the kingdom – those who continued in the legacy of their ancestor David and those who would fail to do so. There were those who totally rebelled against the legacy – Abijam (I Kings 15:3) and Ahaz (II Kings 16:2, II Chronicles 28:1). There were also those who honored the legacy but failed to fully appropriate it in its totality – Asa (I Kings 15:11) and Amaziah (II Kings 14:3). And there were those who latched on to the legacy and allowed it to pilot their lives and reigns – at least, to some degree. These legacy descendants included such impactful leaders as Hezekiah (II Kings 18:3, II Chronicles 29:2), Josiah (II Kings 22:2-3, II Chronicles 34:2), Rehoboam (II Chronicles 11:17), and Jehoshaphat (II Chronicles 17:3).

David's impact was so powerful that generations after his death God made decisions about how He would deal with the nation based not upon the current situation in the country but upon the impetus that King David had set in motion. First Kings chapter eleven recounts the story of how Solomon's wives turned his heart from the Lord and he began to worship the pagan gods that they had introduced in Israel. The anger of the Almighty was kindled against Solomon, and He proclaimed that the kingdom would be torn away from Solomon's hand. "Yet," God added, "for the sake of thy father David, I will not do it during your lifetime. And for the sake of My servant David, I will give one tribe to your son to continue your lineage." (I Kings 11:12-13, 32-36) In the days of Abijam, God considered removing the lamp of the Davidic line from Jerusalem; again, because of His vow to David, God showed mercy and extended the house of His servant. (I Kings 15:3-5)

When Jehoram brought the wicked Athaliah into the royal family, God considered total destruction of Judah; yet, His promise to King David again stayed His hand. (II Kings 8:19, II Chronical 21:7) When the Assyrian general Sennacherib surrounded the city of Jerusalem in the days of Hezekiah, it was, again, for the sake of David that God spared the city and the Judean king. (II Kings 19:34 and Isaiah 37:35) Hezekiah's life was also extended because of God's covenant with David. (II Kings 20:5-6) Eventually, the situation in Israel became so blatantly wicked that God did release His wrath upon King Jehoiachin (Coniah). God ultimately declared that no man of his seed would ever sit on the throne of his father David. (Jeremiah 22:28-30) Had God finally forsaken His promise to establish the house of David? No! Read on. Only five verses later, the prophet declares,

> Behold, the days come, saith the LORD, that I will raise unto David a righteous Branch, and a King shall reign and prosper, and shall execute judgment and justice in the earth. (Jeremiah 23:5)

The prophet Amos also resounded this promise when he spoke of the restoration of the tabernacle of David (Amos 9:11-12), a promise confirmed in the New Testament to be a prophecy of the coming of Jesus. (Acts 15:16)

Let's step back to the invasion of Jerusalem by the Assyrian king Sennacherib to see if we can glean a little insight into what went on behind the scenes to activate the deliverance of the city. Imagine with me the scene.

His eyes glaring and nostrils bulging, the messenger screamed out his threats. He recited a litany of his victories in one ravaging campaign after another, terrifying the people and belittling their ability to defend themselves against this mighty war machine that was camped just outside the city gates. Mockingly, he threatened that any assistance that could possibly be summoned from their allies would be like trusting in a paper tiger to come to their defense. His terrorization continued by ridiculing their faith in God to save them and even suggesting that it was God Himself who had sent him to destroy them. Everyone in the range of his voice knew that his threats were valid; after all, their nation was already buckling under the iron fist of his tyrannical rule to the point of robbing every gold and silver coin from not only the public treasury but also the coffers of the temple and even to stripping the gold plating from the sanctuary doors to satisfy the aggressor's greed and avarice.

Only one man out of the whole nation – an otherwise faceless, voiceless, unknown "nobody" of history – was chosen to go out and face this raging bully. But on this one occasion, Eliakim the son of Hilkiah stepped out of the shadows to take a significant place in the forefront of the saga of his country's destiny. Eliakim stood squarely in the face of the aggressor and challenged him to stop speaking in the Hebrew language but to rather use the native language of the Assyrians because all the top officials of Israel understood the tongue of their oppressor. Rabshaken retorted that it was his deliberate intention to speak in the language of the common foot soldiers in order to strike fear into them as well as to intimidate the executives and bureaucrats. He even punctuated his decree with the prediction that by the time his dastardly deeds were done these poor men would be reduced to eating their own dung and drinking their own urine. Then, in an apparent attempt to incite rebellion and insubordination, he offered the soldiers the option of desertion from the ranks and surrender to his forces with the promise of a peaceful, prosperous life.

Eliakim returned to King Hezekiah and testified of the desperate plight that loomed over the nation. Quickly upon the heels of his report came a letter from Rabshaken's potentate, King Sennacherib of Assyria, spelling out the certain destruction that he planned to carry out upon Jerusalem. It was at that moment that the prophet Isaiah stepped forward with a word of comfort that was soon fulfilled as an angel of the Lord waged supernatural war against the Assyrian army, taking out one hundred eighty-five thousand of them and causing the decimated remnant of the army to retreat without even touching the sacred capital.

Even though nothing earthshaking, pivotal, or miraculous took place during the small part that Eliakim played in this episode of Israel's history, it still seems significant that he was chosen to be the one man who marched boldly onto center stage as this drama was unfolding. And we must ask ourselves why he was chosen and what was the import of the role he played. The answer can be found in the words of the same prophet who foretold the decimation and withdrawal of the Assyrian army:

> And it shall come to pass in that day, that I will call my servant Eliakim the son of Hilkiah: And I will clothe him with thy robe, and strengthen him with thy girdle, and I will commit thy government into his hand: and he shall be a father to the inhabitants of Jerusalem, and to the house of Judah. And the key of the house of David will I lay upon his shoulder; so he shall open, and none shall shut; and he shall shut, and none shall open. And I will fasten him as a nail in a sure place; and he shall be for a glorious throne to his father's house. And they shall hang upon him all the glory of his father's house, the offspring and the issue, all vessels of small quantity, from the vessels of cups, even to all the vessels of flagons. (Isaiah 22:20-24)

In this prophecy, it becomes clear that the reason Eliakim became the man of the hour at this particular moment in history was that he seemed to have a unique God-given, level-headed, unwavering confidence and trust in God in the face of the tumultuous situation. The importance of his role was to establish a sense of stability in the people – and the unique quality or characteristic that qualified him for this role was that he was the one with the key of David. Eliakim's historic role is recounted twice –

in II Kings chapters eighteen and nineteen and again in Isaiah chapters thirty-six and thirty-seven. In both records, the specific reason given for the deliverance of the city was that it was for the sake of David. (II Kings 19:34 and Isaiah 37:35) In some way, Eliakim stood in the stead of David and held his key. Eliakim's significant contribution was the stance he took against the Assyrian messenger who tried to intimidate the people of Jerusalem into surrendering to his army. Eliakim stood up to this intimidator with faith and confidence in God until the Lord caused the invading army to miraculously retreat.

Although the scriptures do not specifically identify what the key of David was, it is easy for us to look back into the life of David and find one characteristic that seems to stand out that could have made the difference between him and any other who lacked this quality. It is likely that we need not go any further than the criteria set for his selection for the throne of Israel. After Samuel had surveyed the seven older sons of Jesse without finding a worthy candidate, the Lord revealed to him that he was looking at the wrong score card when evaluating his options. God made His point that the heart of the matter is actually the matter of the heart.

> But the LORD said unto Samuel, Look not on his countenance, or on the height of his stature; because I have refused him: for the LORD seeth not as man seeth; for man looketh on the outward appearance, but the LORD looketh on the heart. (I Samuel 16:7)

David obviously understood that this was his key to success and determined to keep his heart in a perfect relationship with his God. "I will behave myself wisely in a perfect way. O when wilt thou come unto me? I will walk within my house with a perfect heart." (Psalm 101:2) Even after he sinned with Bathsheba and had her husband killed, the king's prayer was that God would re-establish his heart before Him. (Psalm 51:10) Consequently, the New Testament characterizes David as being a man after God's own heart. (Acts 13:22)

King David desired to pass this spiritual key on to his son Solomon who was to succeed him on the throne. First Chronicles 28:9 records David's instructions to Solomon that he should serve the Lord with a perfect heart. In verse nineteen of the following chapter, we find David in prayer for his son, interceding that the Lord will give him a perfect heart. Unfortunately, the biblical summation of Solomon's life is that "his heart was not perfect with the LORD his God, as was the heart of David his father." (I Kings 11:4)

Second Chronicles 25:2 records that Amaziah did that which was right in the sight of the Lord, yet not with a perfect heart. He was passionate in his campaign to stamp out idolatry, yet he failed to passionately pursue the Lord Himself. Because of this he, like Asa before him, failed to obtain what is likely the greatest promise in the scripture: "The eyes of the LORD run to and fro throughout the whole earth, to shew himself strong in the behalf of them whose heart is perfect toward him." (II Chronicles 16:9) This is the universal blessing and promise of intervention by God that can only be unlocked with the key of David – a perfect heart before the Lord.

It was the promise extended to the church at Philadelphia in Revelation 3:7, which says that the key of David was activated upon their behalf. One unique quality that we notice about the church at Philadelphia is that of all seven churches addressed in chapters two and three of the Apocalypse they are the only congregation indicated as having any relationship to the Word of God. Not only that, they are twice commended for their faithfulness to God's Word. (verses 3:8, 10) Though all seven churches are admonished to hear what the Spirit is saying, apparently only this one listened and heeded. Like David, they recognized that the key to having a perfect heart was to hide God's Word in their hearts. (Psalms 119:11) For them – and for us – the key to the kingdom is a passionate love for the Word of God.

Eliakim apparently had the same heart attitude of love for and confidence in God – the key of David. With that key, he could stand squarely in the face of terror and have faith until he saw the enemy retreat in defeat, humiliation, and terror. David was considered to be a man after God's own heart (Acts 13:22) even though he had so many moral failures. His prayer of repentance in the fifty-first Psalms explained why. His plea before God was that the Lord would not take the Holy Spirit from him and that He would renew a right heart within him. Apparently David understood the necessity of what Paul would later describe as the seal of the Holy Spirit (Ephesians 1:13, 4:30) – the quickening work of the Holy Spirit that constantly reminds the sensitive believer of the validity or lack thereof of his every thought, motive, and action.

Jeroboam

Jeroboam proved himself to be an industrious young man and a mighty man of valor in the courts of Solomon; therefore, the king elevated him to a position of authority in the nation – not knowing that he would eventually rise up against the royal family. However, this threat was dramatically foretold when the prophet Ahijah the Shilonite approached Jeroboam outside Jerusalem and – grabbing his brand new tunic – began to rip it into shreds. Handing Jeroboam ten of the twelve pieces of his former vestment, the prophet proclaimed that God intended to rip the kingdom out of the hand of Solomon and take ten of the twelve tribes to make a separate nation under Jeroboam's leadership. The prophet went on to say that, for the sake of His covenant with David and His prophetic determination concerning Jerusalem, God would preserve the city and two tribes under the leadership of the Davidic house. Once Solomon got wind that a subversion might be in the works, Jeroboam was forced to flee into Egypt until the monarch's death. At that point, he returned to Jerusalem to confront the heir to the throne. The scripture does not make it clear as to what Jeroboam's motives were, but his tactic was to approach Rehoboam with a tax-relief proposal. It is possible that Jeroboam could have had totally altruistic motives in suggesting a way for the new king to gain favor with the people and, therefore, preserve unity in the kingdom. However, in that he already had a prophetic word concerning the demise of the national unity, it is likely that Jeroboam had the ulterior motive of forcing the new sovereign's hand so that he could make his own move toward taking the part of the kingdom that had been promised to him. Regardless of the motive, the end result was exactly what we could have anticipated – Rehoboam refused to lessen taxes and actually increased them, forcing the tribes that were away from Jerusalem to rebel while the people in the vicinity of the capital (where all the tax money was flowing into) reaffirmed their loyalty to the Davidic house. The whole scenario flung the door full open for Jeroboam to walk in and take the reins of the ten northern tribes – fulfilling the words of the prophet!

Knowing that he would never have the full loyalty of his subjects as long as they continued to travel to Jerusalem to worship in Solomon's temple, Jeroboam knew that he had to come up with an alternative to temple worship. His plan was to build smaller shrines in the northern kingdom and encourage the people to sacrifice and worship at them rather than to feel obligated to journey all the way to Jerusalem to worship in Solomon's temple. No matter how logical the approach might have seemed humanly, God considered it an immediate abandonment of true worship and an adopting of paganism and idolatry. He, therefore, sent one of His prophets to confront the new king. This unnamed prophet, known only as "a man of God," was commissioned to go from Judah to the city of Bethel where Jeroboam had set up an altar and to confront the king as he participated in burning incense. His prophecy was to go on and specifically name a child to be born in the family of David generations later who was to destroy the altar and burn human bones upon it. To confirm the validity of his prophecy, the man of God was to call for an immediate sign – that the altar would split apart and that the ashes upon it would pour out upon the ground. When the man of God executed his divine mandate, King Jeroboam pointed toward the prophet, directing his men to arrest him. Miraculously, the king's arm became paralyzed in place so that he could not move it until he begged the man of God to intercede to the Lord for the restoration of the use of his hand.

Chapter fourteen of I Kings tells an intriguing story of the interaction between King Jeroboam and the prophet Ahijah. When the prince fell ill, Jeroboam sent the queen to inquire of the prophet about the boy's destiny. Even though Jeroboam had refused the word of the man of God who had dramatically confirmed his prophetic utterance with miraculous signs and even though Jeroboam was actively promoting idolatry in the nation, he chose a true prophet of God as his source when he needed a supernatural intervention. Assumedly because of his public promotion of paganism, the king asked his wife to disguise herself and go on a secret mission to Shiloh to speak to the prophet. Since Ahijah was blind, there was no real need for the masquerade in trying to fool him; therefore, the ruse was apparently to keep anyone who might discover the purpose of the mission from exposing the king's hypocrisy. Even though the prophet could not see physically, he had perfect spiritual sight – an attribute that resulted in the custom of calling prophets "seers" at this point in history. (I Samuel 9:9) Because of this keen ability of discernment, the prophet knew who was at his doorstep and the purpose of her visit even before he answered the knock on his door. After shocking her by revealing her identity that was doubly hidden – by her disguise and by his blindness – the prophet sent her on her way with more of a message than she had bargained for:

> Go, tell Jeroboam, Thus saith the LORD God of Israel, Forasmuch as I exalted thee from among the people, and made thee prince over my people Israel, And rent the kingdom away from the house of David, and gave it thee: and yet thou hast not been as my servant David, who kept my commandments, and who followed me with all his heart, to do that only which was right in mine eyes; But hast done evil above all that were before thee: for thou hast gone and made thee other gods, and molten images, to provoke me to anger, and hast cast me behind thy back: Therefore, behold, I will bring evil upon the house of Jeroboam, and will cut off from Jeroboam him that pisseth against the wall, and him that is shut up and left in Israel, and will take away the remnant of the house of Jeroboam, as a man taketh away dung, till it be all gone. Him that dieth of Jeroboam in the city shall the dogs eat; and him that

dieth in the field shall the fowls of the air eat: for the LORD hath spoken it. Arise thou therefore, get thee to thine own house: and when thy feet enter into the city, the child shall die. And all Israel shall mourn for him, and bury him: for he only of Jeroboam shall come to the grave, because in him there is found some good thing toward the LORD God of Israel in the house of Jeroboam. Moreover the LORD shall raise him up a king over Israel, who shall cut off the house of Jeroboam that day: but what? even now. For the LORD shall smite Israel, as a reed is shaken in the water, and he shall root up Israel out of this good land, which he gave to their fathers, and shall scatter them beyond the river, because they have made their groves, provoking the LORD to anger. And he shall give Israel up because of the sins of Jeroboam, who did sin, and who made Israel to sin. (I Kings 14:7-16)

With the agonizing reminder that he had been placed in the position of the king over ten of Israel's twelve tribes by the express prophetic word of the Lord and that he had made a one-hundred-eighty-degree turn away from God and had led the entire nation down this perverted path with him, the prophet then declared doom upon Jeroboam, his family, and the nation as a whole. Punctuating the whole message was the death of the boy as soon as the mother crossed the threshold of their home.

In Jeroboam, we see an example of a man who knew in his heart that the Lord is the true God but fought against that awareness "tooth and toenail." He knew that he was placed in power through the prophetic word of the Lord and he knew that he would have to go to a prophet of God when he needed an accurate prophecy concerning his son's life; however, all the while he was hell-bent on eradicating worship of that true God out of his regime and actually set a benchmark that was constantly referred to when measuring the idolatry that would permeate the rest of his nation's history. In much the same way that David became the standard for godliness, Jeroboam became the yardstick for measuring ungodliness and paganism. Generations followed either totally in the devastating clutches of his legacy – Baasha (I Kings 15:34, 16:2), Omri (I Kings 16:19, 16:26), Ahab (I Kings 16:31), Ahaziah (I Kings 22:52), Jeroboam II (II Kings 3:3), Jehu (II Kings 10:29, 10:31), Jehoahaz (II Kings 13:2, 14:24), Jehoash (II Kings 13:11), Zachariah (II Kings 15:9), Menahem (II Kings 15:18, 15:24), Pekah (II Kings 15:28) – or at least partially in ensnared in its grasp – Hoshea (II Kings 17:2).

Jeroboam's negative legacy is summed up in three different references in scripture.

> And he shall give Israel up because of the sins of Jeroboam, who did sin, and who made Israel to sin. (I Kings 14:16)
> Because of the sins of Jeroboam which he sinned, and which he made Israel sin, by his provocation wherewith he provoked the Lord God of Israel to anger. (I Kings 15:30)
> For he rent Israel from the house of David; and they made Jeroboam the son of Nebat king: and Jeroboam drave Israel from following the Lord, and made them sin a great sin. For the children of Israel walked in all the sins of Jeroboam which he did; they departed not from them. (I Kings 17:21-22)

Vanity of the Mind –
Crippler of Legacy

In describing the influence that Jeroboam had upon the people of Israel, II Kings 17:15, uses one significant key word – vanity.

> And they rejected his statutes, and his covenant that he made with their fathers, and his testimonies which he testified against them; and they followed vanity, and became vain, and went after the heathen that were round about them, concerning whom the Lord had charged them, that they should not do like them.

In Ephesians 4:17, Paul directed the believers that they not walk in the vanity of their minds as the gentiles do. Of course, it is easy to immediately define vanity as "emptiness" and go on – totally missing what this verse really has to say. To really catch on to what Paul was trying to communicate, we need to review the book of Ecclesiastes where Solomon defined exactly what vanity entails. In verse 1:14, he concluded that all the works or accomplishments that have been done under the sun are vanity. In verse 2:1, he summarized pleasure and entertainment as vanity. In verse 2:11, he concluded that all forms of employment are nothing more than vanity. Intelligence and education find their way to the vanity list in verse 2:15. Verse 2:17 embraced all of life as vanity. Being in a position of management or authority is also vanity according to verse 2:19. Being in a position to leave behind a legacy or inheritance is also vanity according to 2:21. Verse 2:23 adds diligence and a strong work ethic to the list. Living a moral life falls into the vanity category in verse 2:26. Being human as opposed to simply being a product of evolution still leaves us in the vanity category according to verse 3:19. Verse 4:4 tells us that "keeping up with the Jones" is also vanity. Struggling to make it "up the corporate ladder" falls in the vanity category in verse 4:7. Actually making it to that lonely place "at the top" is also vanity according to verse 4:8. Verse 4:16 describes even the "Rocky syndrome" of the underdog making unexpected achievements as vanity.

Even with all the aspects that we've already mentioned, we are still far from finished with Solomon's list of vanities. Verse 5:10 pulls fiscal security into the discussion of vanity. Verse 6:2 amplifies this truth by adding that – even when it is obvious that wealth is a blessing from God – it can be fleeting and, therefore, vanity. Even long life and a prominent family do not ensure that one's life doesn't end as vanity according to verse 6:4. Verse 6:9 adds desire to the vanity list. Verse 7:6 adds a fool's comments. The inequities between good men and evil men fall on the vanity list in verse 7:15. Verse 8:10 tells us that the things that are forgotten as soon as our obituaries are written are nothing but vanity. The fact that just men seem to get the rewards of the unjust and vice versa is obviously vanity according to verse 8:14. Verse 9:9 says that even a happy home can belie the underlying vanity of the relationship. Verse 11:8 adds that even a long life can be only a camouflage for vanity under the surface. Youthfulness makes the list in verse 11:10. And the concluding summation is that everything is vanity is found in verse 12:8.

That leaves us with essentially "no stone unturned." Business, industry, finance, education, politics, religion, entertainment, family – every area of human interest and endeavor is included as being vanity. Thus, it becomes obvious that the Apostle Paul wasn't saying that the gentiles don't have anything in their brains; rather, he was trying to tell us that the things that they occupy their minds with have no substance. Even if their plans and schemes move nations, transfer fortunes, and change the course of history, they are still vanity in God's sight. Jeroboam actually had the building of a strong nation on his mind when he set up the shrines in Bethel and Gad; however, those grand plans drew him away from his acknowledgement of God – producing inside him a vain mind, empty of any substantial knowledge. Through the legacy idolatry that he perpetrated on the succeeding generations, he enslaved them in this same vanity.

In that nothing is left off of the vanity list, we must question what it is that must be planted so that our minds as believers will not be focused on such vanity? Paul answered this question by sharing his own testimony, "Though I might also have confidence in the flesh. If any other man thinketh that he hath whereof he might trust in the flesh, I more: Circumcised the eighth day, of the stock of Israel, of the tribe of Benjamin, an Hebrew of the Hebrews; as touching the law, a Pharisee; Concerning zeal, persecuting the church; touching the righteousness which is in the law, blameless. But what things were gain to me, those I counted loss for Christ. Yea doubtless, and I count all things but loss for the excellency of the knowledge of Christ Jesus my Lord: for whom I have suffered the loss of all things, and do count them but dung, that I may win Christ." (Philippians 3:3-8)

In this passage, Paul gives us a pretty impressive list of accomplishments and pedigrees that would certainly qualify as the "stuff" of success in almost every dimension of life. Yet, he says that all these things are essentially dung – vanity, if you prefer a little more polite description – to him. The one thing that he says is worthy of his consideration is "the excellency of the knowledge of Christ Jesus my Lord." The truth is that the New Testament abounds with confirmations of the fact that the knowledge of God is the essence of the Christian life. (Romans 1:28, 10:2, 11:33; I Corinthians 15:34; II Corinthians 2:14, 4:6, 10:5; Ephesians 1:17, 3:4, 3:8, 3:19, 4:13; Colossians 1:10, 3:10; II Peter 1:2, 1:3, 1:8, 2:20, 3:18)

It is the knowledge of our Lord and Savior Jesus Christ that must be planted in us to take the place of the vanity that will otherwise fill the thoughts of our minds and hearts. (Ephesians 3:17 Colossians 1:23, 2:7) But does this mean that we must always go about thinking about God and Jesus like monks cloistered away from the rest of the world in a monastery somewhere? No – a thousand times no! We must find a place of balance where we can continue to live in and have an influence upon all the dimensions of society – yet not be sucked into the vacuum of their emptiness. (John 17:15) The key is to realize that Christ is the true essence of every aspect of life – business, industry, finance, education, politics, religion, entertainment, family, and every other element of life. (I Corinthians 8:6, Ephesians 1:10, Colossians 3:11) The exquisite "Christ hymn" of Colossians 1:14-20 expresses this truth with such grandeur:

> In whom we have redemption through his blood, even the forgiveness of sins: Who is the image of the invisible God, the firstborn of every creature: For by him were all things created, that are in heaven, and that are in earth, visible and invisible, whether they be thrones, or dominions, or principalities, or powers: all things were created by him, and for him: And he is before all things, and by him all things consist. And he is the head of the body, the church: who is the beginning, the firstborn from the dead; that in all things he might have the preeminence. For it pleased the Father that in him should all fulness dwell; And, having made peace through the blood of his cross, by him to reconcile all things unto himself; by him, I say, whether they be things in earth, or things in heaven.

Knowing Christ involves much more than mental assent to the truths that we know about Him. Knowing goes far beyond simply hoping or wishing that God is on our side; it involves an unquestionable assurance that comes from actually experiencing the reality of His life in us and our life in Him. Let's look at another passage that demonstrates the all-important role of our knowledge of Christ,

> For though we walk in the flesh, we do not war after the flesh: (For the weapons of our warfare are not carnal, but mighty through God to the pulling down of strong holds;) Casting down imaginations, and every high thing that exalteth itself against the knowledge of God, and bringing into captivity every thought to the obedience of Christ. (II Corinthians 10:3-5)

For many years, I interpreted this passage to mean that God had given us spiritual weapons to pull down the strongholds established in our lives by thoughts that exalted themselves against the knowledge that God existed – ideas like atheism that says there is no God or Hinduism that says that Vishnu, Krishna, Ganesh, or any one of the other millions of their deities is God, or Buddhism that claims Gautama to be divine, or even New Age that tells us that we all are gods. However, the "Ford Better Idea Light Bulb" came on one day when I realized that the serpent in the Garden of Eden did not challenge God's existence; he simply coerced Eve to accept an inferior view of Him. Before the conversation with the devil in snakeskin, Eve knew God as totally benevolent; after allowing the insinuations of the enemy to infiltrate her thinking, she began to suspect that God had a hidden agenda. She allowed a thought that exalted itself against the true knowledge of God to take a toehold in her mind. Before the conversation was over, it had established a stronghold in her heart, and she was ready to betray Him.

The same is true with each of us, if we allow thoughts that are contrary to the biblical revelation that God is our healer, our provider, our righteousness, our victory banner, and our all-in-all to take root in our minds, we will soon believe that distortion and lose our faith and our relationship with Him. Psalm 78:41 says that the people of Israel limited the Holy One of Israel by not remembering how He had delivered them from Egypt. They allowed thoughts that minimized their God to dominate their minds. If we want to think about God properly, we must always be careful to magnify (Psalm 69:30) rather than to minimize Him and His love for His children. Allow me to define "magnify." When we put a specimen under a microscope or examine it with a magnifying glass, we don't actually change its size; all we do is alter our ability to see it. Magnifying has nothing to do with the reality; it only has to do with correcting our inability to see what already exists. Therefore, when we magnify the Lord, all we are doing is adjusting our view of God.

The Holy Spirit helped me adjust my focus one day when He prompted me to realize that I still harbored thoughts that exalted themselves against God. He questioned me as to what I knew about God. I responded by reciting the redemptive names of God. The Holy Spirit then replied that any time I thought that my healing was in the medicine cabinet I was actually entertaining a thought that was exalting itself against what I knew about Jehovah Rapha and that every time I thought that my provision was in asking my boss for a raise I was again entertaining thoughts that exalted themselves against the true knowledge of Jehovah Jireh – and so on. We can go through all the redemptive names and qualities of God to learn what we should be thinking about God. Any time we allow thoughts contrary to these truths into our hearts, we have permitted the enemy to use his deceit to begin a stronghold in our minds. Of course, we all know that God exists, but we fail to attain the true knowledge of who God is and what He does.

> Be not conformed to this world: but be ye
> transformed by the renewing of your mind,
> that ye may prove what is that good, and
> acceptable, and perfect, will of God.
> (Romans 12:2)

The Apostle Peter opened his second epistle with a dramatic contrast – offering us two radically different options: the knowledge of God or lust, "Grace and peace be multiplied unto you through the knowledge of God, and of Jesus our Lord, According as his divine power hath given unto us all things that pertain unto life and godliness, through the knowledge of him that hath called us to glory and virtue: Whereby are given unto us exceeding great and precious promises: that by these ye might be partakers of the divine nature, having escaped the corruption that is in the world through lust." (II Peter 1:2-4)

If we choose to pursue the knowledge of God, we are promised an end result of becoming partakers of the divine nature. In other words, the very DNA of God will be evident in our lives. If we chose to pursue lust, it will end in corruption (putrefied ruination). Interestingly, the apostle adds the special Greek prefix epi to both "knowledge" and "lust" making both words intensive so that they should be read "all-encompassing knowledge" and "all-encompassing lust." Think about how your epidermis, or skin, covers your whole body. In the same way that no part of your body is left without a covering of skin (epidermis), no part of our lives should be left without a covering of the knowledge of God (*epignosis*). Just as we are vulnerable to infection if the epidermis is punctured or cut, our spiritual lives are endangered if we are not blanketed with the knowledge of God. The apostle leaves us with no middle ground – either we whole-heartedly seek God, or we will be overwhelmingly swallowed up with lust, greed, and an ever-spiraling desire for more and more material possessions.

An insightful glimpse into this scenario of never-ending escalation of self-centeredness came when a reporter asked a billionaire how much would be enough. With a little twinkle in his eye, the financier responded, "Just a little more." In similar fashion, we as Christians must become possessed with an insatiable desire for the knowledge of God rather than a self-centered desire for the things of this world. In the immediately following verses, Peter admonishes the believers to diligently pursue maturity by adding layer upon layer to our spiritual lives, ending with a warning that to fail to do so would result in becoming barren and unfruitful in the knowledge of Christ.

Paul presented the identical options in Galatians 6:7-8 when he said that we will reap everlasting life if we sow to the spirit, but corruption if we sow to the flesh.

This all-encompassing knowledge of God is more about <u>how</u> we think about God, not <u>what</u> we think about Him. The issue is not just a matter of knowing that He is all-powerful, but of understanding that He is using this unlimited power to bring blessing and benefit into our lives. We know that God is omniscient – all knowing. However, we can apply that knowledge about His omniscience in different ways. We can assume that since He is all knowing that He knows about all our failures. In this case, we will live our lives in condemnation and defeat. On the other hand, we can apply our knowledge about God's omniscience with an awareness that He knows the intents of our hearts and understands that they are much more noble than the outward failures He has seen. With this in mind, we live victoriously and free of self-condemnation. The key is in <u>how</u> we think about <u>what</u> we know.

Proverbs 23:7 proclaims, "As he thinketh in his heart, so is he." Notice that Solomon uses the word "as" indicating that it is how we think – not what we think – that determines who we will be. If what we think about were the determining factor, all American boys would become convertible sports cars by the time they were sixteen; by the time they were twenty-one they would all have turned into girls; and they would all become a million dollar bills by age thirty. In raising my sons, I was keenly aware that my role as their father was to guide them in <u>how</u> to think. Thinking <u>about</u> cars would never make them actually become automobiles, but the <u>way</u> they thought about cars would determine the kind of drivers they would become. I knew that I needed to focus on helping them think of cars as something other than toys, status symbols, and weapons – otherwise, it would be dangerous to be on the road at the same time with them. Thinking <u>about</u> girls would never make them actually become women, but the <u>way</u> they thought about girls would determine the kind of husbands they would become. I knew that I needed to focus on helping them think of girls as something other than sex objects or ego enhancers – otherwise, they would become abusive husbands with no hope of happy, stable marriages. Thinking <u>about</u> money would never make them actually become dollar bills, but the <u>way</u> they thought about money would determine the kind of spenders and investors they would become. I knew that I needed to focus on helping them think of money as a tool to accomplish their goals and as seed for sowing into the future – otherwise, they would be facing a future characterized by unhealthy greed and debilitating debt.

The way we think about God will radically determine the way we live our lives. When I was working in a campus ministry in the 1970s, I traveled – almost like a circuit-riding preacher – from campus to campus, leading Bible study groups. In one of the groups I visited every couple of weeks, there was a young man who was confined to a wheelchair. When I challenged him to believe God for his healing, he said that he felt that God had put him in the wheelchair to keep him humble. I responded, "Keeping us humble is the work of the Holy Spirit, not a wheelchair." That idea was too radical for him to take, so I admonished him to think and pray about it until my next visit. By the time I returned, he had taken the time to reconsider his view of God and now believed that God was a healer, not one who made His subjects sick. When I prayed for him, strength instantly came into his legs, and he was able to abandon the wheelchair altogether! He had been more crippled in his mind than in his legs!

This student's physical healing can serve as an illustration of the crippling effect that vanity – a mind empty of the true knowledge of God – can become a crippling force in our own lives and the legacy that we are to leave.

Retraining the Heart for Legacy

> For to be carnally minded is death; but to
> be spiritually minded is life and peace.
> (Romans 8:6)

I often imagine a light switch when I read this passage. When we flip the switch up, the lights come one; when we flip the switch down, darkness invades. The same is true in our three-dimensional lives – the body, soul, and spirit. When our soulical dimension (our mental capacity, our determinate will, and our emotional personality) is connected to the spiritual dimension (the part of us that is communication with God), we have positive spiritual life. When we connect our soulical man (also referred to in the scripture as our mind or our heart) with the carnal nature (the physical part of us that is associated with the things of this world that Solomon concluded to be only vanity), the result is darkness, death, and destruction. We see this principle plainly in the lives of David and Jeroboam. David determined to make his heart perfect toward God – and this became the foundation of his positive legacy. Jeroboam, on the other hand, rejected all that he knew about God in order to build a kingdom for himself – and this became the groundwork for his destructive legacy. Thus, it can be concluded that the key to establishing a legacy is to learn how to educate and orient our soulical nature.

Educators tell us that we learn by two methods: emotional implantation and repetition. When a very powerful event happens in our lives, the lesson—whether positive or negative – associated with that event is imprinted solidly on the blackboard of our memories and becomes almost impossible to erase. On the other hand, anything which is repeated often enough – whether true or false – will also become indelibly etched on our memory bank and we wind up believing it whether we really want to or not. The two learning models are basically the same as the evolutionist's versus the creationist's view of the birth of the Grand Canyon. The evolutionist says that the gorge was carved by a little bit of water over a long period of time. The creationist says that the canyon was produced in a very short period of time by a huge amount of water. Whether it is a little thought constantly repeated over a long period of time or a huge thought impacting instantly, the result is all the same—awesome landmarks in our mental and emotional landscape.

Realizing that we can become just as susceptible to remembering and believing the negative and false as we are to being impregnated with the positive truth of the Word of God, we must learn how to guard our thinking so that we do not believe a lie and be damned (II Thessalonians 2:11-12) or, at least, be stunted in our spiritual development.

The Apostle Paul wrote in Romans 12:2 that the key to living lives which are not conformed to the nature of the world but are in alignment with the good, acceptable, and perfect will of God was to be found in renewing our minds – our soulical nature also known as the heart. Jesus told us to be careful how we hear, implying that we must censor not only what we hear but also the mindset with which we hear and the filters which we force the message through before we allow it to impact our lives. (Luke 8:18) Two people can hear exactly the same words with two totally different interpretations because of their predetermined disposition. For example: if we hear that the stock market is going down, one man will hear the news as a warning that it is time to sell and get out of the market before the bottom drops out; another will hear the news as a message that it is time to buy as much stock as possible because it is selling at bargain-basement pricing. Both heard exactly the same facts and figures, but each interpreted them differently because of his personal bias.

Remember the story of the twelve spies who went to check out the Promised Land. Of the dozen men who explored the territory, only Caleb and Joshua ever got to actually live in the land and enjoy its bounty. All twelve saw the land and thought that it was a wonderful place, which flowed with milk and honey. However, two of the men had a different way of thinking about the land, its inhabitants, and – most importantly – themselves. It was how they thought that made the difference. Ten saw the land and thought that it would swallow them up (Numbers 13:32); two thought of the land as God's generous provision (Numbers 13:27). Ten saw the giants and thought that they were too big to hit (Numbers 13:28); two saw them and thought that they were too big to miss (Numbers 13:30). Ten saw themselves as grasshoppers (Numbers 13:33); two saw themselves as well able to take the land (Numbers 13:30). All twelve of these men were chosen for this recognizance mission because they had leadership qualities (Numbers 13:2). In today's standards, they would have all been Ivy League graduates with perfect SAT scores. But only two actually developed into leaders. The difference was all in their minds – the way they thought about the facts they learned.

In Corinthians, Paul addressed the issue of maturing (or failing to mature) when he flatly stated that it was the church's carnality that kept them at the baby stage. (I Corinthians 3:1-3) Later, he told them that it was possible to move forward in maturity and gave himself as an example of one who had put away childish thinking in order to mature (I Corinthians 13:11) and commanded them that they too abandon immature thinking and understanding (I Corinthians 14:20). To the Colossians, he wrote that they could become the new men that God wanted them to be through proper knowledge. (Colossians 3:10) A similar injunction to the Ephesian church (Ephesians 4:23-24) is preceded by a warning that it is those who remain as children who will be deceived by false and deceptive doctrine (verse 4:14). The Apostle Peter (I Peter 2:2) and the author of Hebrews (Hebrews 5:11-12) use the metaphor of food – progressing from a baby's sustenance of milk to a mature person's diet of meat. This emphasized the necessity of solid instruction in the Word of God as the formula for spiritual growth and maturity.

Both Paul and Peter, the two outstanding pillars of the early church, admonish us to establish solid thought patterns as a key to our spiritual survival and maturity.

And be not conformed to this world: but be ye transformed by the renewing of your mind, that ye may prove what is that good, and acceptable, and perfect, will of God. (Romans 12:2)

Wherefore gird up the loins of your mind, be sober, and hope to the end for the grace that is to be brought unto you at the revelation of Jesus Christ. (I Peter 1:13)
Simon Peter, a servant and an apostle of Jesus Christ, to them that have obtained like precious faith with us through the righteousness of God and our Saviour Jesus Christ: Grace and peace be multiplied unto you through the knowledge of God, and of Jesus our Lord, According as his divine power hath given unto us all things that pertain unto life and godliness, through the knowledge of him that hath called us to glory and virtue: Whereby are given unto us exceeding great and precious promises: that by these ye might be partakers of the divine nature, having escaped the corruption that is in the world through lust. And beside this, giving all diligence, add to your faith virtue; and to virtue knowledge; And to knowledge temperance; and to temperance patience; and to patience godliness; And to godliness brotherly kindness; and to brotherly kindness charity. For if these things be in you, and abound, they make you that ye shall neither be barren nor unfruitful in the knowledge of our Lord Jesus Christ. But he that lacketh these things is blind, and cannot see afar off, and hath forgotten that he was purged from his old sins. Wherefore the rather, brethren, give diligence to make your calling and election sure: for if ye do these

things, ye shall never fall: For so an entrance shall be ministered unto you abundantly into the everlasting kingdom of our Lord and Saviour Jesus Christ. (II Peter 1:1-11)

In order to get an insight into how this maturing process actually works, allow me to suggest that you think back to your childhood and remember the little Mister Potato Head toy. Well, since you saw him last, he has grown up, been to Bible school, and is now ordained into the ministry. He is now, Minister Potato Head and he has some important messages to communicate through the little push-in facial features that give him his characteristic appearance – little plastic body parts that make holes in his potato head.

When I was growing up in the Deep South, we used an expression to describe things that we really didn't want or need: "I need that like I need a hole in my head." Even though I'm not sure where the expression came from or what it meant exactly, I want to use that old expression to convey the opposite of what it communicated back when I was a kid. The next few thoughts are as necessary to our spiritual maturity as having some holes in our heads. You see, there are three gateways to the heart that are entered through the holes in our heads. If we can understand how these gateways work and how they interact with our hearts, we will realize the value of the holes in our heads. Our ultimate goal will be to become like the three little monkeys who speak no evil, see no evil, and hear no evil – able to leave a positive and fulfilling legacy.

When we enter a room, we readily realize that it is hot, cold, or comfortable. If it seems a bit chilly or a little warm, the first thing we do is check the thermometer to see what the temperature is. In our personal lives, our mouths are the thermometers of our hearts. Jesus Himself told us:

O generation of vipers, how can ye, being evil, speak good things? for out of the abundance of the heart the mouth speaketh. (Matthew 12:34)

A good man out of the good treasure of his heart bringeth forth that which is good; and an evil man out of the evil treasure of his heart bringeth forth that which is evil: for of the abundance of the heart his mouth speaketh. (Luke 6:45)

Think of any bottle that you might purchase in the supermarket. When you open the cap and start to pour out the contents, the only thing that comes out is what's inside. I'm sure that you are thinking that this is such an obvious truth that it is strange for me to take the space to even mention it. However, have you ever stopped to consider that the opening in the top of the bottle is called its "mouth"? If the bottle has pure water in it, only pure water will come out of its mouth. If the bottle contains poison, only poison will come out through its mouth. The same is true with our mouths; what is in our hearts will eventually spill out through our lips. Just as a thermometer tells us whether the furnace is working, our mouths are true indicators of what the spiritual temperature is inside our hearts.

When the fire of the gospel is roaring full blast inside our hearts, the thermometer of our mouths will soar upward. The prophet Jeremiah testified, "Then I said, I will not make mention of him, nor speak any more in his name. But his word was in mine heart as a burning fire shut up in my bones, and I was weary with forbearing, and I could not stay." (Jeremiah 20:9)

On the alternate end of the spectrum, the Apostle James taught us that the mouth can also become a raging fire if the flames of hell itself are boiling in the heart:

My brethren, be not many masters, knowing that we shall receive the greater condemnation. For in many things we offend all. If any man offend not in word, the same is a perfect man, and able also to bridle the whole body. Behold, we put bits in the horses' mouths, that they may obey us; and we turn about their whole body. Behold also the ships, which though they be so great, and are driven of fierce winds, yet are they turned about with a very small helm, whithersoever the governor listeth. Even so the tongue is a little member, and boasteth great things. Behold, how great a matter a little fire kindleth! And the tongue is a fire, a world of iniquity: so is the tongue among our members, that it defileth the whole body, and setteth on fire the course of nature; and it is set on fire of hell. (James 3:1-6)

Notice that in the middle of this discourse, the apostle mentioned the relationship between our tongue and becoming perfect or mature; conformed to the image of Christ.

Of course, it is true that we can sometimes guard our speech so that what is inside our hearts is not revealed. We've all had those moments when we had to "bite our tongues." However, I have observed that there are two situations in which the secrets of the heart are revealed. The first is in a sudden stressful moment. Just think about the last time you hit your thumb with a hammer or when some careless driver cut in front of you in traffic, almost causing an accident. I'm sure that you even shocked yourself with some of the words that erupted from your lips. The other time is when we are on the opposite end of the emotional spectrum – when we are relaxed and in a totally comfortable, non-threatening environment. I have personally experienced this scenario all too often with ministers as they have gathered for private fellowship after the church service. Men, who just minutes before were preaching faith and love, will often be overheard expressing their doubts and verbalizing criticisms. The relaxed atmosphere of stepping out from in front of the crowd had opened up the gateway of their hearts to expose their true spiritual temperature.

In Psalms 141:3, David expressed his desire to guard his mouth and even acknowledged that his lips were a gateway, "Set a watch, O LORD, before my mouth; keep the door of my lips." However, it is in the following verse that we see that the true heart of the matter is the matter of the heart. "Incline not my heart to any evil thing, to practise wicked works with men that work iniquity." His son Solomon confirmed that the heart is the source in Proverbs 4:23, "Keep thy heart with all diligence; for out of it are the issues of life." Even though he also wrote that life and death are in the power of the tongue (Proverbs 18:21), Solomon acknowledged that the very wellspring for those issues of life is in the heart of the man.

Jesus gave a very thought-provoking teaching when He admonished us to cut off our hands if they offend us and to pluck out our eyes if they cause us to sin. (Matthew 5:30) If we were to follow this teaching explicitly, I'm afraid that the entire church would be populated with blind amputees. However, even those of us who are not able to translate Greek and exegete the text like Bible scholars can sense that the Master must not have been demanding that we begin to mutilate our bodies over every sinful thought or deed. We somehow instinctively understand that Jesus meant that the wickedness resided not in the physical member of the body, but in the sinfulness of our hearts – exactly what Jesus confirmed in Matthew 15:19. The truth is, that if it is too cold or hot in a room, the thermometer cannot alter the situation; the problem has to be dealt with at the furnace. So it is with our lives; our mouths are neither our problem nor the solution. They are only indicators of what churns in the heart. Any correction must come in the heart.

I'd like to quote a couple of lines from a song that my mother often sang to me:

Be careful little eyes what you see,
Be careful little ears what you hear.

If the mouth is the thermometer of our heart, our eyes and ears can be considered to be the thermostats of the heart. No matter what we do to the thermometer, it will not alter the condition of the furnace; however, we can change what is happening in the furnace by adjusting the thermostat. In the same way, what we allow to enter through our eyes and ears will affect the temperature of our hearts.

As Christians, we obviously know that the first and foremost thing which we need to allow to enter our inner man is the Word of God. Jesus said that His words were spirit and life. (John 6:63) If we want life to flow out of our hearts, we must ensure that life is flowing in. The only way to do this is to make sure that we are constantly getting a steady diet of the Word of God. Just one example of the life-giving power in the spoken Word of God can be seen in the vision given to the prophet Ezekiel who was commanded to prophesy to a field of dead bones.

> Again he said unto me, Prophesy upon these bones, and say unto them, O ye dry bones, hear the word of the LORD. Thus saith the Lord GOD unto these bones; Behold, I will cause breath to enter into you, and ye shall live: And I will lay sinews upon you, and will bring up flesh upon you, and cover you with skin, and put breath in you, and ye shall live; and ye shall know that I am the LORD. So I prophesied as I was commanded: and as I prophesied, there was a noise, and behold a shaking, and the bones came together, bone to his bone. And when I beheld, lo, the sinews and the flesh came up upon them, and the skin covered them above: but there was no breath in them. Then said he unto me, Prophesy unto the wind, prophesy, son of man, and say to the wind, Thus saith the Lord GOD; Come from the four winds, O breath, and breathe upon these slain, that they may live. So I prophesied as he

commanded me, and the breath came into them, and they lived, and stood up upon their feet, an exceeding great army. (Ezekiel 37:4-10)

Imagine the power that the Word of God can have in our lives if it can have such a dramatic effect on the totally dead, dismembered, decayed, and dried out corpses of a long-forgotten army. Unfortunately, all too many of us refuse to truly hear and absorb that life-giving Word. In the same context in which Jesus made His proclamation concerning His words being spirit and life, many of His followers turned away because they found His teaching to be too difficult and too demanding. When Jesus turned to His close disciples and asked if they would also abandon Him, Peter responded, "Lord, to whom shall we go? thou hast the words of eternal life." (John 6:68) Even when the truth becomes a "hard pill to swallow" we must determine that we will not forsake it because the Word of God is the only ingredient that can properly fuel the furnace of our faith.

Hindrances to
Becoming a Person of Legacy

Also, no matter how much we try to adjust it, if the thermostat is faulty we won't get any results from the furnace. In the spiritual realm, we can have defective hearing, which will short-circuit the effectiveness of the Word of God. There seem to be several basic hearing problems that plague the human race. The first one is that we simply can't hear from God because we don't belong to Him. Jesus addressed the religious Jews of His day plainly, "He that is of God heareth God's words: ye therefore hear them not, because ye are not of God." (John 8:47) The second condition is spelled out in Hebrews 5:11 where the recipients of the letter were addressed as being dull of hearing, "Of whom we have many things to say, and hard to be uttered, seeing ye are dull of hearing." I'm sure that all of us have sat through lengthy lectures and seemingly-unending phone calls until we reached the "saturation point" where words seemed to begin to flow in one ear and out the other. We may be able to afford putting our brains in neutral on a few such occasions, but not when it comes to hearing the Word of God. Jesus warned us to be careful about not only what we hear but also about the very way we hear, "Take heed therefore how ye hear: for whosoever hath, to him shall be given; and whosoever hath not, from him shall be taken even that which he seemeth to have." (Luke 8:18)

We have to be careful as to <u>how</u> we hear because humans have selective processing, the tendency to hear what we want to hear. I've seen this demonstrated time and time again as I've had students giving reviews of the class that I had just taught. It never ceases to amaze me how so many students hear so many things that I never said in the lectures. Their minds were programed to one frequency and they could only hear that particular message no matter what was actually said in the class. Perhaps this is the reason that the New Testament repeats the command, "He that hath an ear let him hear," at least fifteen times. God gave us spiritual ears to hear what He is saying to the churches, but it is up to us to keep them tuned in and sensitive to His voice. In the parable of the sower, Jesus demonstrated that the Word of God could be sown into unproductive fields with no lasting result or that it could fall into fertile soil and produce an abundant harvest. Interestingly enough, He concludes His remarks with one of the admonitions concerning having listening ears, implying that the ear is the key to having the productive soil for the Word of God. In other words, the ear can be the thermostat that raises the temperature of the heart! (Luke 8:8)

A missionary friend of mine in the Dominican Republic had a problem with the portable generator he needed for a crusade he was doing. When none of the local mechanics could figure what was wrong with the machine, my friend resorted to calling a friend of his on the cell phone. By simply listening over the phone to the sound that the generator was making, the mechanic was able to diagnose the problem with the generator and explain to the missionary what needed to be done to get it working properly. Now that's what I call an attentive ear! God is looking for people with that same kind of spiritual hearing. That's why He insisted to each of the seven churches in Revelation at if anyone has an ear he should hear what the Spirit is saying. In addition, He gave us that same admonition at least nine times during His earthly ministry. (Matthew 11:15, 13:9, 43; Mark 4:9, 23, 7:16, 8:18; Luke 8:8, 14:35)

James warned us that we must not be forgetful hearers (James 1:25) who hear but not with an attentive ear that causes us to remember and act upon His instructions. In verse twenty-two, James explained that the root cause of such hearing problems lies not in our ears themselves but in the fact that we deceived ourselves – a malady that Jeremiah described as being a condition of the heart

(Jeremiah 17:9). James also made a parallel statement when he equated heart deception with an unbridled tongue. (James 1:26) He made another intriguing comment concerning wicked men, saying that they nourish their hearts as in the day of slaughter. (James 5:5) Many translations render this phase to fatten the heart, but a couple make it even more graphic: "indulged your fancies" (Twentieth Century New Testament) and "stupefied yourselves with gross feeding" (Weymouth's New Testament). So what is the bottom line? Our human inclination is to be so self-absorbed that we can't control our lips or our ears. We can be so self-focused that we simply can't force ourselves to talk about the things of God or listen purposefully when He tries to talk to us.

The third hindrance to hearing the Word of God is that sometimes we simply don't want to hear it! Let's look at the story of the giving of the Ten Commandments in Exodus chapter twenty. Verse one plainly states that God orally spoke the Decalogue in the hearing of the entire camp of Israel. However, if we continue the story as it is recorded further on in the chapter we will see that the people begged Moses to become an intermediary between them and God. They did not want to continue hearing directly from the very mouth of God. Instead, they devised a plan wherein Moses would hear the direct voice of God and then communicate His messages to them second-hand. They simply did not want the responsibility of hearing directly from God. I assume that they – just as we often tend to be – were more comfortable with a second-hand gospel because they knew that there might be a margin of error if it passed through a human channel, giving then an excuse for continuing in their unrighteousness. On the other hand, if they heard from the divine source directly, they would be without an excuse.

> And all the people saw the thunderings, and the lightnings, and the noise of the trumpet, and the mountain smoking: and when the people saw it, they removed, and stood afar off. And they said unto Moses,

Speak thou with us, and we will hear: but let not God speak with us, lest we die. And Moses said unto the people, Fear not: for God is come to prove you, and that his fear may be before your faces, that ye sin not. And the people stood afar off, and Moses drew near unto the thick darkness where God was. And the LORD said unto Moses, Thus thou shalt say unto the children of Israel, Ye have seen that I have talked with you from heaven. (Exodus 20:18-22; also see Deuteronomy 5:22-27 and 18:16)

The fourth complication is that we often can't recognize God's voice when He speaks to us. The lad Samuel had this difficulty when God first spoke to him. In the third chapter of I Samuel we find the story of how the Lord called him three times before he finally recognized that it was God Himself calling rather than his mentor Eli. However, if we read the rest of the story, we will see that Samuel subsequently developed an exceptionally clear ability to recognize the voice of the Lord. He became known as a "seer" because he could hear the whisperings of God concerning even the most secret of divine mysteries. In fact, the people of the region actually developed a fear of him, always cognizant that he might "read their mail" and expose the "skeletons in their closets" or reveal the "dust that they had swept under the carpet."

As in the case with the people of Samuel's day who were afraid that he might reveal their transgressions and shortcomings, the fifth reason why we cannot hear the voice of God is because we are simply afraid. This has been a common problem since "day one." It was fear that drove Adam and Eve into hiding and away from their daily time of fellowship and conversation with God. (Genesis 3:8-10)

The sixth problem we have in not being able to hear the Lord is that we often do not give diligence to what we hear. In Exodus 15:26 the Lord, speaking concerning our health and healing, said that we must diligently hearken to His voice and give ear to His commandments in order to partake of His divine provision. While Deuteronomy chapter fifteen speaks of release from financial and physical bondage, verse five limits these provisions to only those who will carefully hearken unto the voice of the Lord and observe all His commandments. The twenty-eighth chapter of Deuteronomy contains an oft-quoted roster of blessings, but we must realize that the opening two verses limit these benefits only to those who hearken diligently unto the voice of the Lord and that verse fifteen turns all the blessings into curses for those who will not hearken unto His voice and observe all His commandments and statutes. For just a minute, let's think on totally natural terms. Suppose you ask someone for directions to a specific place. Imagine that the instructions are a bit complicated with several turns, some to the left and some to the right. If you listen with only a casual ear, you will likely make the first turn with no difficulty and possibly take the second turn correctly; however, by the time you are at the third crossroad, you will be confused as to which way to turn. You'll probably be totally lost before reaching the fourth road. Unfortunately, we are all too satisfied turning a nonchalant car to God and, therefore, missing the precise plan He wants to lay out for our lives. Think of the detail that God gave Moses when He laid out the plans for the Old Testament Tabernacle; it took seven full chapters of Exodus (chapters 25-31) to spell out the pattern for the structure and the priestly order. But, more importantly, notice the preciseness with which Moses followed each detail when he implemented the blueprint. (chapters 36-40) The reward for this attention to detail was an invasion of the presence of the Lord so overwhelming that Moses was not even able to enter the Tabernacle. (Exodus 40:34-35)

We must learn that God is not in the habit of giving suggestions; rather, He gives direct commands that He expects to be followed explicitly. However, we will never be able to follow them in minute detail unless we learn to listen with diligence. I remember being in a service when a prophetic word came forth in which the Spirit reiterated three times that the Lord is God and that His people should kneel before Him in worship. As soon as the prophecy had ended, the moderator of the meeting took the podium, "We've all heard the Holy Spirit's admonition, so let's stand up and praise the Lord." Fortunately, I was in a position of leadership within the group so that it was not out of order for me to step up and correct the moderator by reminding the people that the Holy Spirit had directed us to kneel – not stand – and to worship – not praise. No matter now sincere he may have been, he was wrong and would have led the people astray because he did not hearken diligently to the voice of the Lord in the prophetic message.

In his reflections as he came to the conclusion of his afflictions, Job remarked, "I have heard of thee by the hearing of the ear: but now mine eye seeth thee." (Job 42:5) These remarks open to us a new vista of understanding concerning another one of our abilities to know God. When we hear, we hear the <u>Word</u> of the Lord; but if we look, we can actually see the <u>Lord</u> <u>Himself</u>! Tragically, there are many hindrances that keep us from actually seeing Him as we need to. Like Adam in the garden, we may simply not want to see Him. (Genesis. 3:10) Or, like Isaiah in his encounter with God that awakened him to the wickedness that poured from his lips, we are afraid that seeing God may sentence us to judgment for our unrighteousness. (Isaiah 6:5) Perhaps we are like Manoah and his wife who feared that such a divine encounter would take their very lives. (Judges 13:22)

The more common malady, however, is the simple fact that all of us are blind to one degree or another. Many of us have taken color blindness tests where numbers are arranged in patterns of similarly colored dots. Depending upon the degree of color blindness we suffer, we will be able to pick out the hidden numbers on some of the pseudo-isochromatic plates but not be able to distinguish the pattern on others. In my own personal case, I have a rather marked degree of color blindness – so much so that my eye doctor once asked me if I had trouble telling the red and green lights apart on a traffic signal. I have also had a few humorous situations occur when I have mistaken objects because I thought them to be a different color, such as the time my wife sent me to pick up her green suitcase. As far as I could tell, all her suitcases are black; therefore, I never figured out which one she wanted.

We also suffer from faulty vision in that our minds actually overrule our eyes in many situations. For example, when we look at optical illusions, our minds make us see things in ways that are actually not true at all. A common illusion shows the drawing of two men on a pair of lines that converge beyond the sketches. Because the lines trick our eyes into thinking that the men are standing on a road that vanishes in the distance, one of the men looks like he is far bigger than then other one. Once we take away the lines, we can readily see that the two sketches are actually the same size.

This physical test for color blindness and the games we play with optical illusions can help give us a little insight into what Jesus meant when He explained that He taught in parables because some people had eyes to see and others did not. Just as we all look at the same dot patterns yet not all of us can see the hidden numbers, only the ones who have enlightened eyes will be able to see the message inside the story.

> Therefore speak I to them in parables: because they seeing see not; and hearing they hear not, neither do they understand. And in them is fulfilled the prophecy of Esaias, which saith, By hearing ye shall hear, and shall not understand; and seeing ye shall see, and shall not perceive: For this people's heart is waxed gross, and their ears are dull of hearing, and their eyes they have closed; lest at any time they should see with their eyes, and hear with their ears, and should understand with their heart, and should be converted, and I should heal them. But blessed are your eyes, for they see: and your ears, for they hear. (Matthew 13:3-16)

When Jesus made His statement about having eyes but not being able to see, He was quoting Isaiah 6:9-12, a significant Old Testament passage which is repeated at least four times in the New Testament. (Matthew 13:14, John 12:39, Acts 28:24-29, Romans 11:7-8) We can begin to understand why we are often unable to see even though we have seemingly perfectly good eyes by looking at a couple of clues Paul left us in his first letter to the Corinthians:

> Which things also we speak, not in the words which man's wisdom teacheth, but which the Holy Ghost teacheth; comparing spiritual things with spiritual. But the natural man receiveth not the things of the Spirit of God: for they are foolishness unto him: neither can he know them, because they are spiritually discerned. (I Corinthians 2:13, 14)

Notice the marked distinction between two contrasting worlds of reality – the natural and the spiritual. In the natural realm, we get human teaching; in the spiritual realm, we get teaching from the Holy Ghost. Paul goes on to say that those who are part of the natural order are unable to receive the truths of the spiritual realm – and, in fact, consider them to be foolishness. In the previous chapter of this same letter, Paul had already pointed out that the wisdom of the gospel is foolishness to the unregenerate. (I Corinthians 1:18) To them, it is foolishness to love your enemy or to give when you are in need. However, as he pointed out in the early part of chapter two, this same message which is foolish to the unsaved is wisdom to the redeemed – a wisdom that is hidden until we are enlightened by the Holy Spirit and, therefore, made perfect or mature.

> And my speech and my preaching was not with enticing words of man's wisdom, but in demonstration of the Spirit and of power: That your faith should not stand in

the wisdom of men, but in the power of God. Howbeit we speak wisdom among them that are perfect: yet not the wisdom of this world, nor of the princes of this world, that come to nought: But we speak the wisdom of God in a mystery, even the hidden wisdom, which God ordained before the world unto our glory: Which none of the princes of this world knew: for had they known it, they would not have crucified the Lord of glory. But as it is written, Eye hath not seen, nor ear heard, neither have entered into the heart of man, the things which God hath prepared for them that love him. But God hath revealed them unto us by his Spirit: for the Spirit searcheth all things, yea, the deep things of God. (I Corinthians 2:4-10)

In his second epistle to this same church, Paul gives two reasons why we have eye problems. The first cause is that our eyes are blinded and the gospel is hidden from us by the devil.

But if our gospel be hid, it is hid to them that are lost: In whom the god of this world hath blinded the minds of them which believe not, lest the light of the glorious gospel of Christ, who is the image of God, should shine unto them. (II Corinthians 4:3-4)

Remember Nicodemus' clandestine interview with Jesus? He wanted to know the secrets of the kingdom of God, and he was shocked to learn that it is impossible to even see the divine kingdom without being born again. (John 3:3) Nicodemus did not understand natural – much less spiritual – things. The god of this world has done such a good job of blinding the eyes of his subjects that they cannot see the kingdom that is presently among them. (Luke 11:20)

The second reason the apostle listed is even more tragic: we have voluntarily put a veil over our eyes. It is one thing to be blinded by an antagonistic force, but it is a totally different matter to willingly blindfold oneself in order to avoid the illuminating light of God. In Exodus chapter thirty-four, we read the story of how the people of Israel asked Moses to place a veil over his face to filter out the blinding glow on his countenance when he descended from his mountaintop sojourn with God. Paul explains the spiritual ramifications of their request.

> And not as Moses, which put a veil over his face, that the children of Israel could not stedfastly look to the end of that which is abolished: But their minds were blinded: for until this day remaineth the same veil untaken away in the reading of the old testament; which veil is done away in Christ. But even unto this day, when Moses is read, the veil is upon their heart. Nevertheless when it shall turn to the Lord, the veil shall be taken away. Now the Lord is that Spirit: and where the Spirit of the Lord is, there is liberty. But we all, with open face beholding as in a glass the glory of the Lord, are changed into the same image from glory to glory, even as by the Spirit of the Lord. (II Corinthians 3:13-18)

God not only shows us the condition and its cause, He also reveals the cure. In His very first sermon, Jesus declared that He was anointed to give sight to blind (Luke 4:18), and His ministry proved that He did in that many blind received their sight – a miraculous ministry that continued under the hands of the disciples after Jesus' ascension to heaven. (Matthew 9:27, 11:5, 12:22, 15:30, 20:30, 21:14; Mark 8:22, 10:46; Luke 7:21, 14:13, 18:35, 24:11; John 5:3, 9:1; Acts 9:12) In His message to the seven churches of

Revelation, the Risen Lord confronted the Laodicean church because they saw themselves as healthy, wealthy, and wise. Jesus, on the other hand, recognized them as needing eye salve to correct their blindness. (Revelation 3:18) The context of His message to the church reveals that this healing is actually repentance – the only cure for both blindness caused by the diabolic work of our enemy and the self-induced blindness resulting from our own willful actions!

If the first step to the remedy is repentance, the subsequent step must be to use what vision we have been given. Remember that Jesus said that His reasoning for teaching in parables was because some were not given the ability to see. To the unregenerate Pharisees, He gave few parables; instead, He pointedly told them to repent. (Matthew 4:17, Mark 1:15, and Luke 13:3, 5) It was to the disciples who were beginning to see properly that He addressed the parables and even agreed to give some explanation of them. When Jesus began to explain the parable of the sower to these disciples, He added that the ones who had such ability would be given even more. (Matthew 13:12) They were the fertile soil in which just one seed of the gospel could germinate and produce thirty, sixty, or even one hundred revelations. In a subsequent discourse, Jesus *emphasized the point.*

> For unto every one that hath shall be given,
> and he shall have abundance: but from him
> that hath not shall be taken away even that
> which he hath. (Matthew 25:29)

Our ability to have spiritual insight will increase if we put it to use. Yogi Beara is quoted as having said, "You can observe a lot by looking." Although he was not a theologian, he seemed to understand a truth that is demonstrated in the Bible. In Acts chapter three, we read the story about the first miracle healing through the church after the Lord's ascension. It is interesting to note the various verbs used to describe the action of seeing. In verse three, the lame man is referred to as "seeing" Peter and

John as they neared the temple. The next verse says that Peter "fastening his eyes" on the invalid, commanded that he "look on" the apostles. Notice the progression in the intensity of the verbs. When the lame man was only <u>seeing</u>, he had no spiritual insight and remained subject to his crippling condition. When the apostle <u>fastened</u> <u>his</u> <u>eyes</u> on the beggar, he focused his attention in a way that he had never done before. It is certain that Peter had noticed this man many times as he had gone in and out of the temple over the years; however, today was different – there was a purposeful awareness that had never been there before. Finally, the afflicted man was directed to <u>look</u> – an action verb conveying purpose and expectant anticipation. That look of faith brought the man out of his physical dimension into the spiritual reality where he was able to receive his miracle. The author of the book of Hebrews also directs us to move from simply <u>seeing</u> the host of faithful witnesses to taking a purposeful focused <u>look</u> at Jesus, the author and finisher of our faith. (Hebrews 12:1-2) The implication is that deliberate and purposeful focusing of our spiritual attention can enhance our ability to see into the things of the spirit realm. Hebrews 5:14 declares that we can develop our senses – suggesting our hearing and our sight – by purposefully using them. If we have become blinded by deliberately placing a veil over our eyes, certainly we can undo that deficiency by concentrated focus.

> But strong meat belongeth to them that are
> of full age, even those who by reason of use
> have their senses exercised to discern both
> good and evil. (Hebrews 5:14)

Paul even numbered himself among those who had limited clarity in vision when he testified in I Corinthians 13:12 that we (including himself) see through a "glass darkly." But he also proclaimed that there was a day coming when we would "see face to face." His point was that we can anticipate total revelation at the final resurrection; however, that resurrection power is already working in and through us today. (Ephesians 3:20)

Additionally, we have the gifts of the Holy Spirit in our present lives as a foretaste of the power of that kingdom to come; therefore, we can expect to grow in clarity of vision as the Holy Spirit enlightens our present understanding. (I Corinthians 2:10) That is why Paul dedicated himself to praying for the church to receive the Holy Spirit's impartation for spiritual vision.

> I cease not to give thanks for you, making mention of you in my prayers; That the God of our Lord Jesus Christ, the Father of glory, may give unto you the spirit of wisdom and revelation in the knowledge of him: The eyes of your understanding being enlightened; that ye may know what is the hope of his calling, and what the riches of the glory of his inheritance in the saints. (Ephesians 1:16-18)

Many – if not most – believers suffer from Christian myopia, a nearsightedness that keeps us from looking at the full picture. Eighty-nine percent of American households own an average of three Bibles, yet fifty-two percent of Americans rarely or never read the Bible and only thirty-three percent say they read the Bible at least once a week. If we don't read God's Word, we will never be able to see the full truth that He wants to reveal to us. Even more significant is that those who do read the Bible often fail to allow the Bible to read them. To genuinely be healed of the spiritual blindness in our lives, we need to allow the light of the truth of the scripture to illuminate the obstacles that have blurred or obstructed our vision. (Matthew 7:3) Some people neglect spending time in study of the scriptures using the excuse that they can't understand so much of it. The truth is that we shouldn't be bothered by what we don't understand in the Bible; rather, we should be concerned about what we do understand but have failed to apply to our lives. Once we begin to seriously read and apply the Word of God, we will discover that our vision gets more and more clear and accurate.

Another application of eye salve comes in a bottle labeled "forgiveness." According to the beloved disciple John, our eyes can be blinded by walking in unforgiveness toward those around us.

> He that saith he is in the light, and hateth his brother, is in darkness even until now. He that loveth his brother abideth in the light, and there is none occasion of stumbling in him. But he that hateth his brother is in darkness, and walketh in darkness, and knoweth not whither he goeth, because that darkness hath blinded his eyes. (I John 2:9-11)

One of the characters in the 1998 movie <u>Patch</u> <u>Adams</u> was a patient in a mental institution whose characteristic behavior was to get into the face of each person he met, hold two fingers in front of him, and demand, "How many fingers do you see?" Of course everyone thought that he was crazy because of this erratic behavior; however, Patch Adams eventually realized what the gentleman was up to. When Patch looked beyond the fingers and gazed at the man himself, the fingers were out of focus. Suddenly, he saw four – not two – fingers! The point of the object lesson was that we need to learn to look at the people whom God places in our lives rather than at the problems they may cause us. If we continue to focus on the problems, we will never see the people as God wants us to see them; we are blinded and walk in darkness.

When God wrote a personal memo on the wall of the Babylonian banquet hall, the devil and all his sorcerers demonstrated their lack of spiritual insight when they tried to read the words that were written plainly before their faces. (Daniel 5:5-29) <u>Mene</u>, <u>mene</u>, <u>tekel</u>, <u>upharsin</u> was a list of the coins in circulation in their empire. They could not go beyond the surface meaning of the names of their coinage. Certainly the Almighty was interested in more than just pocket change in His personal visit with the leaders of a great empire. Only Daniel – with his ability to understand what everyone else was simply looking at – was able to see that the name of each coin also had a second meaning. Just as our term "nickel" means a five-cent coin but also names a kind of metal, mene meant "to measure" in addition to naming their currency. Just as our term "quarter" means "one fourth" in addition to naming our twenty-five-cent coin, tekel had a second meaning of "to weigh." Like our term "half" signifies the fifty-cent coin as well as meaning "fifty percent," pharsin [u is the term for "and"] meant "to divide" as well as designating a monetary value. The terms mene and pharsin also seemed to suggest the rising empire of the Medes and Persians. All this revelation was "as plain as the handwriting on the wall," but the magicians were blind to it.

The most tragic of all shortsightedness would be failing to see God when He is present and active in our lives.

> Philip saith unto him, Lord, shew us the Father, and it sufficeth us. Jesus saith unto him, Have I been so long time with you, and yet hast thou not known me, Philip? he that hath seen me hath seen the Father; and how sayest thou then, Shew us the Father? (John 14:8-9)

As both a preventative and corrective measure for this kind of spiritual blindness, the scripture continually commands us to diligently and purposefully seek God. For those who seek the face of God, the most popular promise is in II Chronicles 7:14, which says that He hears from heaven and will forgive their sin and will heal their land. Psalm 24:4-6 says those who seek the Lord have clean hands and a pure heart and are in line for blessings and righteousness from their God.

Whether we will be able to see the Lord depends on the condition of our hearts. "Blessed are the pure in heart: for they shall see God." (Matthew 5:8) Certainly, the pure in heart will see God in "the sweet by and by" of our eternal abode, but the truth is that we can begin to see Him in the "bitter here and now" of our temporal residence. Moses had this privilege (Exodus 33:11), but this was also extended to all the people of God.

> And they will tell it to the inhabitants of this land: for they have heard that thou LORD art among this people, that thou LORD art seen <u>face</u> <u>to</u> <u>face</u>, and that thy cloud standeth over them, and that thou goest before them, by day time in a pillar of a cloud, and in a pillar of fire by night. (Numbers 14:14)

I know that it seems that we have had a long and rather tedious journey since the illustration of flipping on the light switch; however, that expedition has eventually brought to the place where we have come face to face with God Himself. It is at that point – and only at that point – that all the vanity and emptiness of our minds can be replaced with the all-encompassing knowledge of God, giving us the opportunity to transformed through the renewing of our hearts and minds into individuals who can leave a positive legacy.

Legacy Lives On

The story is told of a New York City news team who uncovered the relationship between two men in their city. One was a homeless man on the streets who always slept over the steam vent beside one of the skyscrapers in the city's business district. The other was a multi-millionaire business magnate whose company occupied one of the luxurious office complexes in the same skyscraper. The surprising connection between the two men is that they were brothers!

When the news crew interviewed the homeless brother, their main question was, "Why did you wind up here on the street?" Without taking even a second to think, the man blurted out an accusation, "My father was an alcoholic and a very abusive man. He doomed me to a life of failure."

Next the team took the elevator to the top of the skyscraper and introduced themselves to the receptionist in the brother's corporate office. After clearing all the formalities, they were ushered into the executive suite where they could interview the president. This time, their question was, "What was the secret behind your success?" Just as quickly as his brother had responded, he was ready with an answer, "I grew up in a home with an abusive and alcoholic father. That experience made me determined to make something out of my life."

There is a powerful lesson to be learned here – the greatest influence in these two men's lives was their father, and they knew it so well that they didn't even have to think about it. The father left a legacy for both of his sons. For one, it was a legacy of doom; for the other, it was the challenge to go out and create his own destiny and start a whole new legacy.

One of the earliest memories I have is that of a preacher (In middle of the last century in the Deep South, we never spoke of the "pastor" – only the "preacher.")

asked me what I wanted to be when I grew up. I remember telling him that I wanted to grow up to be like Papa Timms, my grandfather. It wasn't until many years later that I learned the backstory to my grandfather's life and discovered that he – like the man in the Manhattan penthouse – had made a decision to change his family legacy.

When my grandfather was barely into his teens, he realized that his parents' lifestyle was not one he could tolerate; so, he collected the few dollars he could get his hands on and walked out the front door of his father's home to start a new life – one that would have no resemblance to the one he was leaving behind. And he did just that! Turning to God as his only source, my grandfather – Harrison "Papa" Timms – eschewed anything that even faintly resembled the environment that he grew up in. Holiness and righteousness were the non-negotiable standards that he and Carrie "Mama" Timms set for themselves and their eleven children. As cotton farmers in upstate South Carolina, they worked hard for every penny they were able to bring in and prayed hard for each of those pennies to stretch far enough to feed the family. Yes, working and praying were two things that they were good at.

Papa had a menial education, but Mama was functionally illiterate – having had to leave school at age ten to work in the cotton mill in order to help support her family. In fact, it wasn't until she had reached the age to start receiving Social Security that she learned how to write her own name so that she could sign her check each month. Yes, life was hard for them, and you could say that all the odds were stacked against them – but they had their two buttresses that saw them through all the hard times – hard work and strong prayers.

In the early 1900s, an unusual phenomenon began to occur around the world. The most well-known manifestation of this phenomenon happened on Azusa Street in Los Angeles, California, but there were similar occurrences happening almost simultaneously around the world – Africa, India, and the backwoods of the

Carolinas. This phenomenon was the outpouring of the Holy Ghost (Back then, the term "Holy Spirit" simply wasn't part of anyone's vocabulary.) with all sorts of supernatural manifestations such as healings, speaking in tongues, and people falling under the power of the Holy Ghost. From this miraculous outpouring, the Pentecostal Movement was birthed and soon swept across the country and around the world. As soon as the revival flames touched the South Carolina foothills where Mama and Papa called home, this hard-working, strong-praying couple readily embraced it.

Those were the so-called "good old days," when automobiles were a rarity, indoor plumbing was unheard of, electricity in the home was a luxury, and telephones, televisions, and most of what we consider necessities today weren't even dreamed of. These were the days when "central heat" meant a coal-burning potbelly stove in the middle of the room and the most fashionable form of transportation was a horse and carriage. It was into these grim situations that the Holy Spirit fell. And fall He did!

He so mightily overpowered the hungry souls that the stories they left behind are almost unimaginable. Papa and Mama used to tell of times when people would "fall out under the power" and land on the red-hot stove but roll off without a single blister! They would talk about times when people would "swoon" – what we would call today, "being slain in the Spirit" – and be in a trace for four or five days. Their family members would have to pick up the effected brothers and sisters and put them on wagons or buckboards and carry them home to wait for them to eventually regain consciousness. Out of this fervent move of God in the lives of my grandparents, was birthed the heritage that I claim today as the legacy that has shaped my life and the lives my whole family.

Back on the farm, Papa had a pattern of going to the barn to pray every day. Of course, when you have eleven children, there is a certain amount of natural solace to be found in hiding in the barn even without the supernatural consolation of spending the time with

God. His prayer list included his entire brood and all who were to come into the family through marriage and birth. Now, when you start off with eleven children and they all marry and have children of their own, you can imagine how that prayer list must have grown and how much time he got to spend in that barn. But the important thing is that his prayers established a heritage and a legacy that reverberated far beyond that barn in Cheddar, South Carolina. When I was married in 1980, my wife was the one hundredth member to become part of the family and a member on Papa's list – even though he had gone on to his spiritual reward years before. I have no estimation on how much more that list has mushroomed in the years since we passed that centennial mark, but I can say that the power of that prayer list has never waned no matter how many years it has been since Papa has been here to physically call out the names, how many names have been added since his pencil has fallen still, or how many of the descents don't even know about Papa or his list.

One of Papa's requests was that none of his family would ever die without knowing the Lord – and I can say that, as far as I know, the Lord has honored that request. We have always seen any wayward members come back to the Lord before their deaths. The family tree has been blessed with an unusual harvest of preachers, Bible teachers, gospel singers, Christian writers, and missionaries. Additionally, even those who did not follow careers in the ministry have made significant contributions in their chosen fields of education and business.

You might have guessed that when Papa and Mama died, they didn't leave behind a fortune to be divvied up among their children. But they left the greatest inheritance that anyone could ever dream of – the godly legacy that prepared the way for us to prosper in this life and enjoy the eternal blessing of the one to come!

When I think of the impact that one godly man can have on not only his family but all the future generations that his descendants touch, I'm reminded of another godly man with eleven children and his world-changing legacy. When a study was done on the heritage of Jonathan Edwards, the Puritan preacher from the 1700s, it was discovered that in one hundred and fifty years following his death, his family had produced one US Vice-President, three US Senators, four state governors, three city mayors, thirteen college presidents, thirty judges, sixty-five professors, eighty public office holders, one hundred lawyers, and one hundred missionaries.

A contemporary of Edward's, Max Jukes, has quite a different legacy. When it was discovered that the family trees of forty-two different men in the New York prison system traced back to him, a study was made that revealed that his family had produced seven murderers, sixty thieves, fifty women of debauchery, one hundred thirty other convicts, and three hundred ten paupers with over twenty-three hundred years lived in poorhouses.

In the concluding chapter of our little study, I want to share a poem that my Aunt Nora's composed as a tribute to Papa. Her closing remarks confirm that Papa and the Wall Street multi-millionaire were worlds apart in the inheritances that they left behind even though both left unspeakable legacies for the future generations – an observation that reminds me of the life of King Solomon. Even though Solomon left behind massive sums of finances (And the king made silver and gold at Jerusalem as plenteous as stones, and cedar trees made he as the sycomore trees that are in the vale for abundance. – II Chronicles 1:15), his money is long gone; yet, his influence lives on in his books of wisdom that remain and have been translated into almost all the languages of the world.

Even though Solomon acknowledged, "A good man leaveth an inheritance to his children's children," (Proverbs 13:22) he was not actually talking about leaving money. At that time in history, there were rules that established that the inheritance had to go to the oldest son – prohibiting the division of the inheritance among siblings, not to mention across generational boundaries. He was saying that we need to leave a legacy of righteousness that can cause each generation to prosper and then have something to pass on after them. The majority of inheritances are gone – either spent or wasted – within six month of the death of the benefactor. But, a good man can leave an influence that makes a difference in the beneficiaries.

I understand that Solomon's wealth was equal to that of the four hundred wealthiest men alive today. But where are Solomon's trillions today? No one knows, but we still have his proverbs and all the other wisdom that can impact our lives and change the world.

One godly person can make a lasting difference and leave an enduring legacy. Join David, Solomon, the New York entrepreneur, and my Papa and make that decision today!

MY PAPA

By: Nora Faye Timms Martin
December 31, 1983

Let me tell you a true story if I can;
A story to me of a great man.
Then just a lad his Pap died,
And to help his mother he really tried.

There wasn't much time for going to school,
But he learned to follow the "Golden Rule."
He said he only finished the Third Reader,
For in the family he had become leader.

In harvest time he would batch with Walt Pepper.
And tales he would tell were as hot as red pepper:
Like cats named "soap and water" doing their dishes,
And some other tales would put you in stitches!

At age twenty-three, and seven dollars in cash,
He and Carrie Lee Morgan really made a dash.
They slipped out of Paris Mountain Holiness Church,
and were married.
When services were over, to her father's house they
were carried.

With seven dollars and a sixteen-year-old wife,
They launched out together on a new life.
But a void in their life they needed to fill,
So they knelt at an altar, and to God their lives did yield.

A calm and a peace now flooded their soul,
With an inner strength to help reach their goal.
The rest of their lives they drew from that strength,
Knowing that from God's power there was all length.

A number of years in a factory he did work,
His duty to his family he never did shirk.
Then back to the farm one day he did go,
For fresh air and sunshine were not his foe.

They had a flock of young ones, twelve in toll,
And every one to him were worth their weight in gold.
He loved, supported, and taught them the best he could;
The way that any God-fearing father would.

There were Troy, Donnie, Lois, Mary, and Nora Faye,
(Her twin died at birth, they named her Dora Mae).
Then came Walter, Clyde, and Hattie Ruth.
That's not the whole crew I'll tell you the truth!

Then came Thelma, Delbert, and Addie Jean.
These all pulling together made a team.
How did he feed and clothe that many, you'd say?
He served a big God, and He made a way.

As a share cropper, he farmed and worked in a store,
With this extra income there would be more
To put aside for a goal he had in his mind,
Someday a farm of his own to find.

On Saturday night when he came home from the store,
Along with the groceries, there would be more:
A bag of scrap candy (fifteen cents it did cost)
And mind you, not a scrap of it would be lost.

One-half gallon of peanut brittle and peppermint sticks
Divided among the eleven kids for them to lick.
This was a treat from Papa every Saturday night:
Mama divided it out around the old lamplight.

Papa was truthful and honest in every way,
"His word was his bond," his fellow man did say.
A life lived like this will really pay,
For some day to all comes a reckoning day.

He saw that we all graduated from school,
That we learned also to follow "The Golden Rule":
For he remembered his school days and the Third Reader,
And hoped that someday his kids would become leaders.

Then finally one day his dream did come true,
There were two houses and an acreage of fifty-two.
He paid cash for this, with the money he had saved,
And this was his home 'till he went to his grave.

The Belton Church of God he did attend,
And taught Sunday school to a class of men.
God gave him an insight into His Word.
He told things of the future we had never heard.

One day the disease of cancer came along.
After his surgery, he was not very strong.
This gave him more determination than ever:
His relationship to God to never sever.

When we'd start on vacation to him we'd go see,
This is the song that he would sing to me,
"So many are taking vacations to the mountains, lakes,
and seas.
When I take my vacation in Heaven, won't you take your
vacation with me?"

Then one day at the age of seventy-eight;
A pain in his heart, it began to ache.
That night at forty-five minutes past eleven,
He began taking that "Vacation in Heaven."

If we knew that he looked down on us today,
Would we do what we do, or say what we say?
Or would we say, "Papa wouldn't want me to do this,"
And never again would take such a risk:

Of never again seeing Papa and the God that he loved,
Or taking a vacation with him up above

(where there is no sickness, no sorrow nor woe.)
So let's all make preparation for to Heaven to go.

Papa didn't leave me fortune or fame.
The wealth that he left me was a good name.
The things of this world are like shifting sand,
But people still speak of Papa as "A Good Man."

Greatness is not measured in dollars and cents,
Nor the people we know, nor the places we went.
It's living for God and NEVER EVER STOPPING.
That's what I call great, AND THAT WAS MY PAPA.

Teach All Nations Mission

Teach All Nations Mission (TAN) is a global evangelical educational ministry birthed from the teaching ministries of Delron and Peggy Shirley. The name for Teach All Nations Mission was chosen to carefully indicate the exact heart of the Shirleys' mission. TAN's commitment is to establish a solid biblical foundation in national pastors and leaders so they can help enrich their own people. This vision is being accomplished by holding national leadership conferences and publishing and distributing Christian teaching materials in English and their local languages.

Someone accurately observed concerning the revival that is occurring in many parts of our world today that it is a mile wide but only an inch deep – the result of energetic evangelism by both missionaries and local Christians. Sadly, there is a marked shortage of teachers who are taking the next step in fulfilling our Lord's directive to teach them how to observe all that He has commanded. Therefore, Teach All Nations Mission has literally taken the words of Christ from Matthew 28:19, "Teach all nations," as its motto and mission statement.

TAN's commitment is to deepen that revival by training the pastors and leaders who then go back and strengthen their congregations. TAN pays for the travel and lodging of handpicked leaders because Delron and Peggy want to invest into their lives but know that these third-world saints could never afford to come at their own expense. TAN always provides the meals for all the guests during these conferences. The ministry also furnishes solid Christian literature in their local language or in English for those who understand the language.

Delron and Peggy realize that the challenge is much bigger than what they can accomplish in person; therefore, they have determined to expand the scope of their vision. One area of expansion includes a scholarship fund that will allow selected individuals to obtain a formal education in solid Christian colleges and Bible schools or through correspondence courses. The ministry has also assisted in building a Christian school in Zimbabwe and a Bible college in Nepal. Additionally, Teach All Nations assists the pastors and leaders they work with in times of need such as the tsunami in Sri Lanka, the earthquake in Nepal, and hurricanes in Belize and in the Turks and Caicos Islands.

Your gifts to and prayers for Teach All Nations will help the Shirleys continue their outreach to Christian leadership around the world.

Teach All Nations Mission
3210 Cathedral Spires
Colorado Springs, CO 8904
719-685-9999
www.teachallnationsmission.com
teachallnations@msn.com

Books by Delron & Peggy Shirley

available at www.teachallnationsmission.com

A New Dawn Rises – Rethinking Christian Struggles
(the second volume in the Non-Conformer's Trilogy)

In <u>A New Dawn Rises</u>, Bible teacher Dr. Delron Shirley examines the accounts of some of the great spiritual struggles in the Bible from Jacob's all-night wresting match with an angel to Jesus' agonizing three hours in the Garden of Gethsemane. The conclusions that he draws from these stories can change the way that you view life and all the challenges it may bring your way.

Becoming a Person of Legacy
(the third volume in the Non-Conformer's Trilogy)

Someone once said that the two most important days of a person's life are the day he is born and the day he discovers why he was born. Each of us has a divine destiny that God has orchestrated since before we were even born. Unfortunately, most people live their whole lives without actually finding – much less, fulfilling that purpose. In <u>Becoming a Person of Legacy</u>, discover how to make your life leave a lasting impact.

Bingo – A Fresh Look at Grace

An old joke tells of a man who stood at the Pearly Gates recounting all his good deeds in an effort to gain entry into Paradise. When Saint Peter tallied up the gentleman's score, he did not have anywhere near enough points to qualify. His knee-jerk reaction to the count was, "I'll never get in except by the grace of God." At that instant, the gates swung open and Saint Peter graciously welcomed the gentleman inside. We all know that it is only through grace that we will ever inherit the kingdom of God, but how

67

much do we understand about this all-important subject? Join Bible teacher Delron Shirley as he explores the biblical principle of grace and investigates some of the misconceptions that are current in the Body of Christ today.

Christmas Thoughts

Christmas. The very mention of the word fills our hearts and heads with thoughts – joyous memories, visions of childhood delights, scenes of family gatherings, smells of fresh pastries, tastes of delicious holiday treats, recollections of special friends, strains of favorite carols, and "warm fuzzies" of evergreens, mistletoe, roaring fires, fancy wrappings, shiny decorations, and happy faces. Yes, Christmas is all about thoughts. And we invite you to snuggle up with a hot chocolate and delve into our thoughts about Christmas – and the Christ child whose coming we are celebrating.

Cornerstones of Faith

In our Christian faith, there are some important cornerstones which serve as foundations to bear the weight of the life we are to build upon them, as indicators or identifiers of who we are as believers, as ceremonial testimonies to the fact that our lives are being built upon Christ, and as unquestionable and invariable standards against which to test and measure everything else in our lives. Proper attention to these essential cornerstones of our faith ensure that our lives rest upon a firm foundation so that we will not fail or falter. Join Delron Shirley in an examination of the foundation on which our lives must be built.

Daily Devotional Bible Study (five volumes)

This five-volume set of studies takes you on a four-year journey through the Bible. Each manual consists of a walk through the scripture based on studying one chapter each weekday for the fifty-two weeks in a year. Each daily entry includes one verse to memorize. Next comes a short distillation of the basic principle of the chapter and a brief outline of the chapter. This study is intended to be of a rather devotional approach. The Bible study is followed by a simple prayer intended to bring the truth of the chapter into practical application. A section for the reader's notes follows where you can log your own personal revelations and insights about the chapter. A space for logging your own personal spiritual journal (which could include prayer requests, answered prayers, and testimonies) rounds out the daily devotion. The entries for the weekends are a similar format for a study through Psalms. Just twenty minutes a day, seven days a week, fifty-two weeks a year will produce one brand new man in each individual who seriously applies himself to the program and the program to himself.

Daily Ditties from Delron's Desk (Six issues are available)

Each new day comes with its own challenges and blessings. In <u>Daily Ditties from Delron's Desk</u>, you'll enjoy a little pick-me-up to get your day started. So sit back with a warm cup of coffee or tea and see what is in store for you today.

Good People, Bad Things, and Vice Versa
(the first volume in the Non-Conformer's Trilogy)

One of the most difficult questions that has challenged ordinary men and the world's greatest thinkers and philosophers throughout the ages has been, "Why do bad things happen to good people and why do good things happen to bad people?" The answer to this conundrum lies in simply reprograming the way we think about inequity and the divine order of things. Join Bible teacher Dr. Delron Shirley as he explores the biblical truths that will help unravel this mystery.

Lessons from the Life of David

Michelangelo's famous sculpture <u>David</u> in the Piazza Signoria in Florence, Italy, has often been noted as a most perfect depiction of the human body. And we often think of its subject – the biblical David – as being perfect as well. However, the wonderful thing about the Bible is that it tells the truth – even about its greatest heroes. They are presented to us as uncovered as Michelangelo's subject, with the only difference being that the Bible depicts its subjects with all their warts, mid-rib bulges, scars, and other defects. In <u>Lessons from the Life of David</u>, Bible teacher Delron Shirley explores both David's triumphs and failures in order to find valuable lessons for our own lives for today.

The Great Commission – DOABLE

While traversing the teeming streets of Kathmandu, Nepal, missionary teacher Delron Shirley was overwhelmed with the throngs of people who had not yet heard the gospel of Jesus Christ. Looking out at the myriad of faces, it seemed like an impossible task to reach them all. Yet, he knew that Jesus' directive was that the gospel be taken to every human—not just in this one city, but on the entire planet. If reaching this one city seemed like a gargantuan challenge, reaching the planet was beyond imagination! Join Delron in his quest through the scriptures as he explores why the Bible promises that the Great Commission can actually be accomplished and how it is doable in our generation.

Dr. Livingstone, I Presume

Probably the most famous quote in all the annals of missionary history is the greeting of newsman and adventurer Henry Stanley when he finally reached missionary and explorer David Livingstone in the remote interior of Africa, "Dr. Livingstone, I presume?" In this little study based on that historic encounter, Bible teacher and missionary Dr. Delron Shirley considers how we can really pick out who is a missionary. His real hope is that you can find yourself in these few short pages and join the call to fulfill the Great Commission of bringing the gospel of Jesus Christ to the whole world in this generation.

Finally, My Brethren

"Finally, my brethren," these are words that seem all too familiar to us when we think of putting on the armor of God for spiritual warfare. However, we often miss the real impact of Paul's message to the church because we have used this as our starting point. But just as we don't start at the top step when we climb a ladder, we can't begin our preparation for spiritual warfare at the last step – putting on the armor. In fact, the Apostle Paul gave us more than fifty steps of preparation to complete before we are ready to get dressed for battle. Join Delron Shirley as he uncovers these often neglected truths. Discover life-transforming truths about your enemy, yourself, God, who you are in Christ, who Christ is in you, and your position in the struggle between the powers of heaven and hell.

Going Deeper in Jesus

In this seventy-three-day devotional volume, Bible teacher Delron Shirley invites you to go with him on a quest into the Jesus treasure chest to discover the unimaginable gifts that God has made available to us in Christ.

The IN Factors

It was offering time in the Sunday school class, and the teacher directed the children to quote a Bible verse about giving as they dropped in their nickels and dimes. A little Afro-American girl with her hair in meticulously cornrow braids grinned from ear to ear as she dropped in the first coin and quoted, "It is more blessed to give than to receive." Her redheaded, freckle-faced friend shyly blushed as she added to the coffer while mumbling, "Give and it shall be given back to you." Next, a young guy tossed in what might have been his "tooth fairy money" as he flashed a broad smile that exposed the spot where his front tooth had been last Sunday. He then recited, "The Lord loves a cheerful giver." As the fourth little fellow stumbled through, "The seed in the good soil brought forth thirty-, sixty-, and one-hundred-fold return," the teacher anxiously eyed the next child – a first-time visitor who had not been schooled in any of the "giving" passages. Anxious over the fact that the guest would be embarrassed, her heart raced a bit as the offering basket reached him. As the reluctant little tyke begrudgingly plunked in his contribution, he blurted out, "A fool and his money are soon parted." Although the visitor's quote wasn't from the Bible, it was apparently more appropriate in his own case than any of the verses with which the teacher had coached the rest of the pupils. The truth is that most of us, like the students in the elementary class, have been taught only part of the lesson of what God wants us to know about finances. In The IN Factors, Bible teacher Delron Shirley invites you to join him as he explores some of the lessons that have been taught – but equally important – truths on the topic.

In This Sign Conquer

Marching toward an enemy that he wasn't sure he could defeat, Constantine questioned himself, his army, his military abilities, and even his deities. Then suddenly something happened that changed his life. No, something happened that changed the whole history of Western civilization. He saw a vision in the sky of the Christian cross accompanied by the words, "In this sign conquer." Abandoning his pagan gods and accepting the cross of Christ as his battle insignia, he marched into the Battle of Malvian, defeated Maxentius, and took the throne of the Roman Empire. Since none of us was there in AD 312, we can't be certain how sincere the new emperor was in his acceptance of the cross as his victory symbol. However, we must know that there are signs and symbols that God has given to each of us to ensure our victory and success in life. Join Bible teacher Delron Shirley as he explores this fascinating topic.

Interface

This book should be viewed as an anthology because each of the seven studies was written at a different time with no deliberate connection to the other six. However, there is a thread running through these independent studies that ties them all together as they communicate different aspects of one unified message – being strategic in our spirituality. The first study deals directly with the interfaces discussed in the Bible where we connect with the world around us, the kingdom of heaven, and the kingdom of darkness. The second study in the series discusses finding the sensitive balance between two necessary interfaces – our need to spend time with God and our mandate to rise up and interact with the world. The third and fourth studies have to do with the biblical truths that we need to understand in order to accurately interface with our God, our world, and ourselves. In the letters to the seven churches of Asia Minor recorded in Revelation chapters two and there, only one of the churches is specifically mentioned as being at an interface; the church at Philadelphia is said to have an open door set before it. Interestingly, this is also the only church that is specifically mentioned as having a relationship with the Word of God. (Revelation 3:8, 10) The fifth study takes us through the life of one of our most beloved biblical heroes—David, the shepherd boy who killed a giant and wrote beautiful psalms. Although his life was riddled with one failure after another, he somehow attained the report that he was a man after God's own heart, which is the key to opening the doors of interface with the world that we learn about in the letter to the Philadelphian church. (Revelation 3:7) Next, we look at what it really means to have a heart after the very heart of God – one that Bob Pierce, founder of World Vision, described as being broken with the same things that break the heart of God. Finally, the book concludes with a challenge to never fall short of the opportunities and blessing that God has provided for us as we interface with the One who sent us and those with whom we are to interface.

Israel – Key to Human Destiny

The Jewish people and the nation of Israel are puzzles and enigmas in world politics and human logic. How can it be that a group of people who account for less than one half of a percent of the world's population is responsible for one out of every five Nobel Peace prizes? Israel is so tiny a territory that no world map can even squeeze its name on the space allotted it on the layout, yet this minuscule nation dominates our evening news every night. Why is it that one little country of only a few million people can tie up the wealth, the foreign policy, and the political movements of the greatest nations on the face of the earth? Why is it that of all the ethnic groups in the world, only one bears the stigma (or honor) of having its name specifically coined into a word of hate and antagonism: anti-Semitism? The answers to these puzzling questions lie in the fact that these are no ordinary people and this is no ordinary piece of real estate. These are covenant people living in covenant land. Their destiny is charted by prophetic words from God Himself. Indeed, the saga of all mankind revolves around this people. Israel is the key to the human drama. Join Delron Shirley as he journeys into the past and glimpse into the future in order to understand the present.

The Last Enemy

Fear? Death? Defeated!! The Bible declares that death is our ultimate enemy and that the fear of death is a cruel warden that can hold us in the chains of slavery and bondage throughout our lives. BUT, our enemy Death has met his Waterloo and can no longer hold us in his power. In The Last Enemy, explore Passover weekend AD 33 changed your destiny.

Lessons Along the Way

Welcome to a journey that will lead you across the towering Himalayan Mountains, over rushing waterfalls, and into your own backyard. At each step of the journey and around each bend in the path, you will discover the most exciting thrills of life – not the rush of adrenalin released while crashing through the rapids of the Grand Canyon, not the spine-tingling chill of coming face-to-face with demonic supernatural forces, not the awesome hush of grandeur inspired by the majestic sunsets across the glacier polish of the majestic Sierra Nevada range – although all these and much more are included. Rather, you will discover the thrill of hearing the voice of God Himself speaking to you for direction and encouragement. Join us on this fascinating journey through life. Be ready to learn all the lessons along the way!

Living for the End Times

"The end is near!" "Jesus is coming back!" "These are the last days!" We all have heard these prophecies. Sometimes, we've heard them so often and over such a long period of time that they may have lost their impact. Yes, we believe that these are the last days, but we somehow keep living as if we think that things will always keep going as they always have and that nothing is ever going to change. Is it possible that we have given mental ascent to the concept of the end time but never let it really get hold of our lives? Let's explore what it means to live our lives as if we really believed that these are the end days – after all, they really are!

Maturing into the Full Stature of Jesus Christ

As a child, I learned a little song in children's church: "To be like Jesus, to be like Jesus. That's all I ask – just to be like Him." When I grew up, I realized that there was a whole lot more to becoming like Christ than just singing a little children's song. It has been said that going to church doesn't make you a Christian any more than sitting in the garage will make you an automobile or sitting in a donut shop will make you a policeman. There is a maturing process that we must go through if we ever hope to manifest the true nature of Christ in our lives. That maturing process demands that we have a total transformation in the way we think – that we be brainwashed, if you will. It requires more than just saying the right words; after all a parrot can speak English, but he is not an Englishman. In the same way, we must not settle for just learning the Christian jargon; we must be transformed into the very likeness of Christ through the renewing of our mentalities. You may not be what you think you are, but what you think – YOU ARE! Join Bible teacher Delron Shirley as he investigates how the way we think determines who and what we will be. Learn how your thinking can transform you into the full stature of Jesus Christ.

Maximum Impact

He showed up totally unannounced with no publicity agent, no campaign manager, and no budget to fund a campaign. Yet within three short weeks, he established a viable community of faith that was soon acknowledged and recognized as a role model throughout the world. Who was this man, and how did he flip the world one hundred eighty degrees on its axis? Join Bible teacher Dr. Delron Shirley as he makes a fascinating quest into the man, his methods, and the mission of a man who left maximum impact everywhere he went.

Of Kings and Prophets – Shapers of the Destinies of Nations

Dr. Delron Shirley invites you to travel back through the corridors of time to visit the era of the Old Testament kings and prophets in the nations of Israel and Judah – the men who shaped the destinies of their nations. In walking through the encounters, interactions, and conflicts in the lives of these historical figures, we are constantly reminded of the words of the New Testament writer who said that everything that happened in the lives of these men serves as an example and a caution to us so we can make a difference in our own generation.

Passion for the Harvest – A Missions Handbook

We all know the Lord's statement that the harvest is plenteous but the laborers are few. However, I would like to suggest a little different consideration of the situation: the harvest is plenteous but the laborers are untrained. The cover photograph of a Nepali woman harvesting her grain not only pictures the primitive conditions in which the third world harvests their physical grain, it also helps us get a glimpse of the need for the entire Body of Christ to be trained for the spiritual harvest as well. <u>Passion</u> <u>for</u> <u>the</u> <u>Harvest</u>, explores some of the pertinent truths necessary for preparing us for the challenge of the harvest. Learn how to sow in order to reap an abundant harvest and how to discern the harvest that the Lord is sending your way. Learn how to develop the resourcefulness and the expectant hope necessary to stand steadfastly until the harvest manifests and we discover new truths concerning the tools and the stamina necessary for reaping the full harvest. In short, develop a passion for the harvest!

People Who Make a Difference

Have you ever noticed that there are some people who just seem to stand out from the crowd? Although they may seem ordinary in so many ways, there is just some special something about them that identifies them as unique individuals. Though they may not be the "movers and shakers" that we think of as the ones who can push their way to the top of the corporate ladder, they somehow wind up leaving an indelible mark on their worlds. Let's explore what it is that makes some people the ones who make a difference. Better yet, let's learn how to be those individuals!

Positioned for Blessing and Power

In the first Psalm, David gave us a formula for a life that qualifies for God's blessings – be careful about where you walk, sit, and stand. In the book of Ephesians, the Apostle

Paul gave us a formula on how to live in the power and authority of God – be determinate about where we sit, walk, and stand. Bible teacher Delron Shirley combines these two principles – one from the Old Testament and one form the New – in a way that can revolutionize your life.

Problem People of the Bible

In <u>Problem</u> <u>People</u> <u>of</u> <u>the</u> <u>Bible</u>, you will meet many of the biblical characters you have had to skip over as you did your daily reading because you simply couldn't understand exactly how their lives figure into the message of God's love and plan of salvation. This insightful story will help you make sense of their place in the grand scheme of the Bible and the story of God's dealings with the human family.

So, You Wanna Be A Preacher

A distillation of Delron Shirley's twenty-five years of mentoring young ministers and the evaluation of over ten thousand church services and sermons, <u>So</u> <u>You</u> <u>Wanna</u> <u>Be</u> <u>A</u> <u>Preacher</u> covers a wide range of topics from how to recognize and respond to the call into the ministry to tips on preparing and presenting your sermons and on getting them published. Special emphasis is given to helping you understand the minister's job description and recognizing how to manifest the Holy Spirit's presence in your ministry. The minister's personal life – including discussion of ethics and etiquette – is a major focus in the study. No matter what your ministry or calling, you are guaranteed to get new insights in your role as a minister and gain some helpful hints into effectively serving the Lord and His people.

Tread Marks

Does your life leave a mark on the people you meet and the circumstances you find yourself in? In <u>Tread</u> <u>Marks</u>, you'll learn a number of where-the-rubber-meets-the-road principles of successful Christian living that are guaranteed

to ensure that you will leave a positive impression on individuals and society. Based on biblical principles and true life experiences, this book grapples with everyday life issues and presents simple but effective approaches to facing them successfully and victoriously. From the stories of the sinking of the Titanic and an African safari adventures to the expositions on Joshua's conquest of the Promised Land and Joseph's rise from slavery to the second most powerful man in Egypt, you'll be entertained, inspired, and motivated. You'll discover how your life can make a lasting impression.

A Verse for the Day (Two Issues are available)

In A Verse for the Day, Bible teacher Delron Shirley brings you a new insight into the Word of God each day with observations about the unique contributions the selected verses can make in our lives. Though the studies of these verses are by no means comprehensive or exhaustive, the fresh insights you'll gain in these daily visits with the Word of God are guaranteed to encourage, challenge, and inspire you in your walk with the Lord.

Women for the Harvest

"God's secret weapon" – that's how many people are coming to realize that we, as women, are in the world of ministry. One example is, Dr. Yonggi Cho, who has the second largest church in the world. He has been quoted as saying, "Women are the greatest evangelistic tools. Someday the church will catch on." In this volume, author Peggy Shirley does an in-depth study into the history of why women have been forbidden from taking their God-given place in the church and explores the powerful biblical and historical examples of what happens when women are allowed to use the giftings which God has placed inside them. A revealing study of the scriptures which have long been used to block women from service, coupled with a motivational study on how to break free from the bondages which have held women back and a wealth of practical suggestions and advice -- this book is guaranteed to release you to become a true laborer in God's end-time harvest.

You'll be Darned to Heck if You Don't Believe in Gosh and Other Musings

This eclectic collection of mediations and musings addresses many issues concerning our Christian faith, including exactly what the Bible teaches about hell and who will go there, how prayer works, and how we should understand exactly who Jesus is. This study also takes you on a spiritual journey that delves into such topics as simple advice for Christian leaders and the biblical formula for radical change – both in your own personality and in the complexion of a whole nation.
Lighthearted at times, but always simple and straight forward, this refreshing study makes discovering theological truths from the scripture fun and enlightening. Buckle your seatbelt as you join Bible teacher Delron Shirley as he journeys to such interesting places as Nepal and Nigeria in quest of spiritual insight and revelation. You'll be glad that you came along for the adventure as you discover many simple truths that have always seemed just too difficult to understand.

Your Home Can Survive in the 21ˢᵗ Century

Have you ever heard someone say that we should get rid of old fashion ideas about marriage, family, and morals and add "After all, it is the twenty-first century"? With the rapid decline in traditional values, we might actually begin to question if our home will be able to survive in this new century. But there is good news if we only recognize that what is happening to the family today is a prophetic attack by the forces of the devil and that we are well equipped to fight back and conquer! Dr. Delron Shirley says, "Your home can not only survive – it can thrive!!"

www.ingramcontent.com/pod-product-compliance
Lightning Source LLC
LaVergne TN
LVHW051153080426
835508LV00021B/2612